Changing Views

art, contemplation & wellness

Edited by Lindsey Hepler

OpenGrounds . University of Virginia

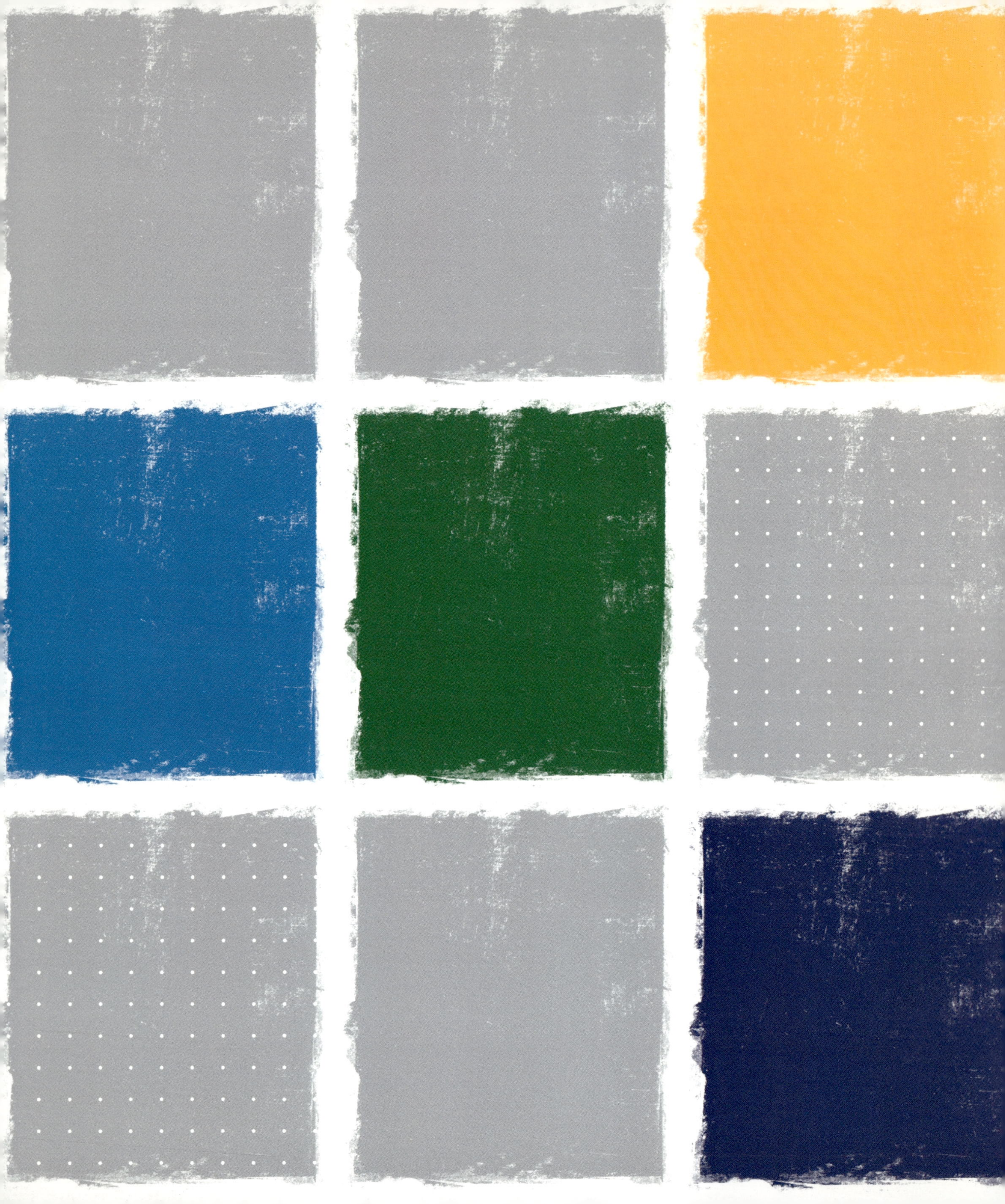

4 **Introduction**
Choreographing Collaboration
Lindsey Hepler

7 **Defining Contemplation**
David Germano

. . . .

12 The Phillips Collection

13 **The Museum as a Contemplative Space**
Klaus Ottmann

19 **Contemplation Audio Tour**
Can Looking at Art be Good for You?
Brooke Rosenblatt

. . . .

26 **Building Bridges across Knowledge Domains**
JD Talasek

29 **Clinician's Eye**
Marcia Day Childress
Jordan Love

34 **Drawing Attention**
Barbara Bernstein

. . . .

40 Music, Consciousness, and Healing

41 **A Course on Music and Consciousness**
Fred Everett Maus

49 **Music Heals**
Katie Somers

51 **Self-Healing with Music Therapy**
Rachel Kim

. . . .

53 **A New Way of Seeing**
Contemplation and Art
Naomi Worth

58 **The Space of Contemplation**
William Sherman

. . . .

62 **Acknowledgements**

. . . .

Introduction
Choreographing Collaboration

by

Lindsey Hepler

Associate Director of OpenGrounds, University of Virginia

As a dance student in college, I learned to choreograph by first learning to improvise. Rather than arbitrarily choosing movements to go with music, I began my exploration with a broad theme and a desire to explore that theme through movement—to embody it. The process could be individual or collaborative. Working as an individual, I would delve deeper into the ideas I sought to explore, understanding them in my own body. Working as part of a group, I would explore ideas and thematic elements as the other dancers and I moved together, composing ourselves in space.

Through improvisation, I learned to choreograph from "the free play of consciousness," making time and space to explore "spontaneous expression." I learned to embrace "the world [as] a perpetual surprise in perpetual motion. And a perpetual invitation to create."[1] I learned about intention and parameters; about creating a safe space for exploration, play, and the suspension of judgment; and about committing to risk taking. I learned how to work with others as we continually generated new material and then adapted and refined the material, over and over again.

It seems important to emphasize that all of this learning was not just taking place in our minds, but in and through and with our bodies. As John Dewey wrote, "Without external embodiment, an experience remains incomplete."[2] Embodied learning (a common characteristic of all forms of artistic expression) creates deeper learning.

OpenGrounds operates from an arts- and design-informed ethos—from the principles of design thinking. The Corner Studio is a space for experimentation and risk taking. Projects develop through a process of collaborative empathizing, defining, ideating, prototyping, and testing. These foundational principles and the ensuing processes are the same as those I learned through improvisation. As such, managing the *Art, Contemplation, and Wellness* initiative became for me an improvisation exercise, an opportunity to choreograph a multi-faceted, multi-institutional collaboration around a shared thematic interest.

OpenGrounds and The Phillips Collection, an "intimate museum combined with an experiment station,"[3] have been collaborating since 2010, jointly convening Design Gatherings, supporting UVA faculty artists, and engaging researchers whose work resonates with current exhibitions. This partnership is based on the recognition that connections between science and art are important building blocks of our future, and the hope that this collaboration between higher education and the learning community of the museum will set the stage for the birth of new ideas.

When *Art, Contemplation, and Wellness* emerged as a theme of mutual interest for both UVA and the Phillips, we seized the opportunity to engage in a more expansive approach to our collaboration. JD Talasek, Director of Cultural Programs at the National Academy of Sciences, was a part of our earliest conversations and offered an opportunity for UVA and the Phillips to jointly present on this topic at the DC Art Science Evening Rendezvous event in February 2015, an important forum for sharing our work and the culminating event for our collaborative exploration. Seeking to tie together public events in Charlottesville and Washington, DC with guest artist visits, course work, and the development of contemplation/meditation tours at both the Phillips and UVA's Fralin Museum of Art, we approached the collaboration with an improvisational spirit. Moving forward from our original impulse, we convened a group of faculty at UVA and encouraged new ideas and collaborators to emerge. Through this approach, we were able to broaden the scope of the project beyond the museum toinclude musicians, studio artists, medical practitioners, and more. Partners from across the university, including the Contemplative Sciences Center, The Fralin Museum of Art, the Center for Design and Health, the Center for Biomedical Ethics and Humanities, and the Compassionate Care Initiative, were engaged throughout the process as we came together to consider art as a meditation and the museum as a meditative space, along with the implications of both art and contemplation for human flourishing. Throughout the initiative, we prioritized direct experience with theideas at hand, seeking to show rather than tell as often as possible.

This book compiles the rich facets of the *Art, Contemplation, and Wellness* initiative into a single work that will give this project a life extending well beyond the direct experiences of the past year. The essays and images contained within, contributed by practitioners, artists, scholars, and students, highlight the intersections between aesthetic experience and human wellness, especially as encountered in the physical space of the museum. They aim to explore both the experience of space and the experience of art within a contemplative framework of understanding, and to demonstrate the role of contemplation in clinical practice and education.

---

1 Nachmanovitch, Stephen. *Free Play: Improvisation in Life and Art.* New York: Jeremy P. Tarcher/Putnam, 1990.

2 Dewey, John. *Art as Experience.* New York: The Berkeley Publishing Group, 1934.

3 Phillips, Duncan. 1926, http://www.phillipscollection.org/about.

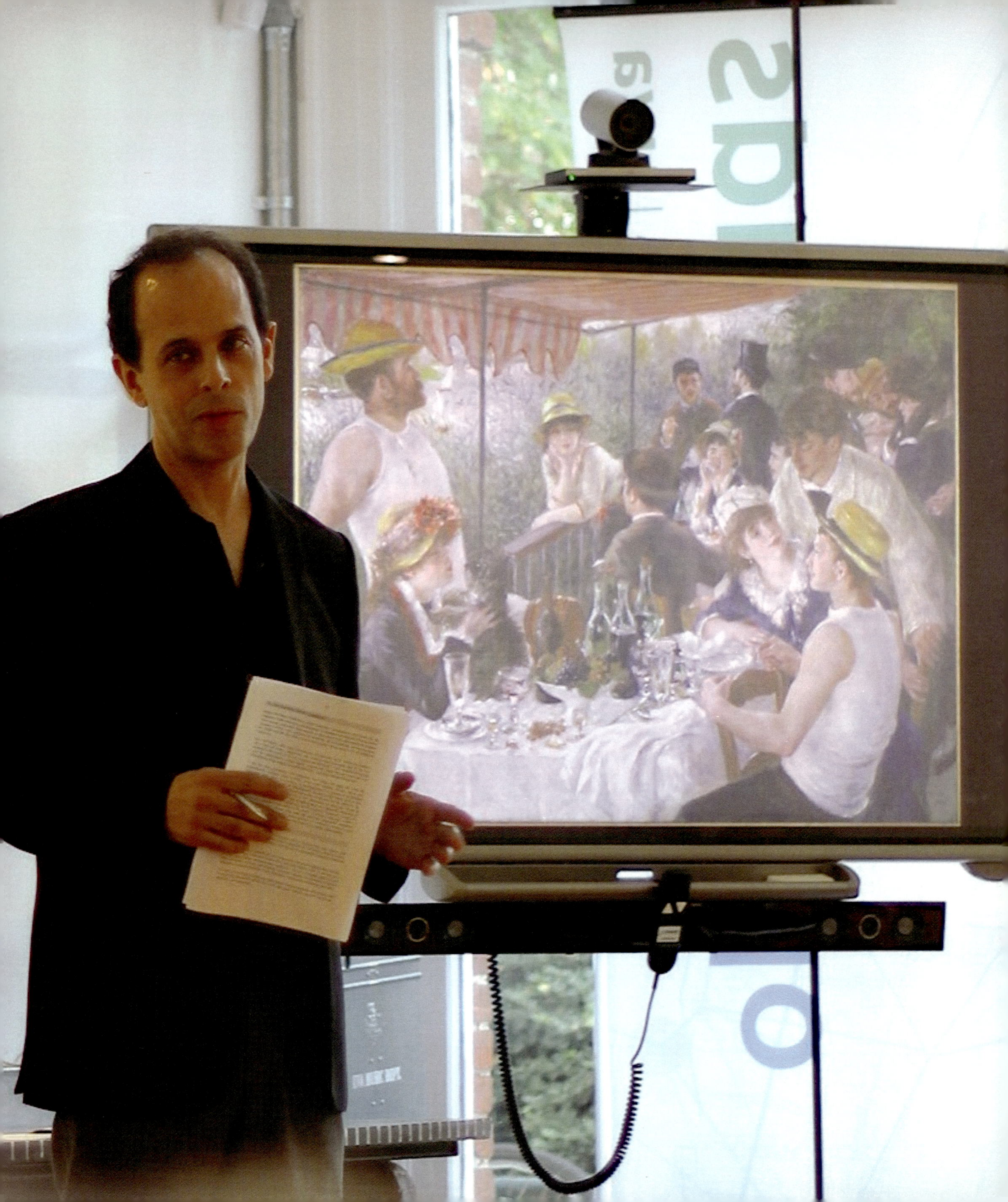

Defining Contemplation

by

David Germano

Director of the Contemplative Sciences Center, Professor of Religious Studies, University of Virginia

My academic life has focused on Buddhist contemplation and philosophy from the start. Yet, as the University of Virginia has recently explored contemplative sciences and considered what contemplation might be in different walks of life—undergraduate education, businesses, healthcare, K-12 education, and so forth—I came anew to the question, "What is contemplation?" Although I knew Buddhist meditation, the way in which everyone was newly talking about contemplation, meditation, mindfulness, and yoga was unclear to me. I began to question what is meant by terms like contemplation, meditation, mindfulness, or yoga in each context. What are the common features of the practices placed under such umbrellas? What are their benefits and dangers in changed circumstances? And what do I mean by it when speaking on behalf of the Contemplative Sciences Center, promoting contemplation in a variety of social sectors?

We should think about contemplation's provenance in religion. We can look at religious traditions and ask questions about history, use of terms, and the variety of practices and experiences involved. In Buddhism, there are practices for empathy cultivation, attention training, visualization and performance trainings, somatic meditations, emulations of dying and sexual experience, lucid and transformative dreaming, and more. It is not clear how these diverse practices and experiences relate to one another, a topic Buddhists have been struggling with for centuries without consensus. Also, what happens when a practice is taken from a religious context—Buddhist, Hindu, Jewish, Christian, Islamic, or Native American—and shifted into a nonreligious context?

If our interest is in contemplation here and now at the University of Virginia and in various social sectors in the United States, we can take an ethnographic perspective and ask how people are using the term. We find a tension between flexible engagement and incoherent generalities in this regard. For example, what does "contemplative" as an adjective mean, as people speak of contemplative parenting, walking, banking, and art, or mindful mayonnaise? What magically happens when we preface such a word to, for example, reading? What is the difference between reading and *contemplative* reading, entrepreneurship and *contemplative* entrepreneurship, nursing and *contemplative* nursing, learning and *contemplative* learning? Or parenting, sexual relationships, museum tours, and so on?

opposite

David Germano presenting at the *Art, Contemplation, and Wellness* kick-off event at the OpenGrounds Corner Studio, September 2014

Photo: Erica Ruth, Class of 2015

It seems everything can benefit from the word "contemplative" or "mindful" prefacing it, but what does it really mean anymore? Prefixing "contemplative" to an ordinary activity to create two forms of the same activity is new in its scale, characteristics, and interrelation with the advertising industry, but there are ancient roots in such transformation of an ordinary activity into an extraordinary activity. Buddhism, for example, renders walking into a contemplative process, as well as dreaming, sexuality, and more. While they have not applied the word "contemplative" in contemporary ubiquitous manner, Tibetan Buddhists have for centuries worked with core human processes and practices in a meditative context.

I like how the term "contemplation" has an extraordinary semantic range, as evidenced in a range of conversations I have had over the past few years. For example, a man who taught soccer to disadvantaged youth said the most important thing he taught was contemplation, namely to take a pause between an emergent situation and the subsequent reaction. When team members are out there on the soccer field and someone elbows them, instead of smashing the person back, they learn to stop for a moment and think, "Okay, what just happened? What am I going to get out of this? What do I want to do?" The coach wanted to make sure they took that contemplative pause to consider the situation before acting, rather than focus on their ultimate reaction. Another example came from a marketing professor who talked about contemplation as wanting his students to take a moment to be reflective about what they were doing and why they were doing it. He felt that if through his teaching and mentoring he could introduce that reflective moment, it could have a transformative impact on those students hell-bent for Wall Street without really considering why, or the values with which they were trying to align. Or there is the nursing school's implementation of a contemplative pause within the operating theater. When someone dies, they take sixty seconds to consider what just happened—a quiet cessation of their transactional activity and a reflection on that person's passing away.

In this amazing spectrum from reflective pauses to complex religious practices, one common thread I have identified from Tibetan Buddhist practices is that contemplation typically has a beginning, a middle, and an end. This is a simple key to understanding contemplation. The beginning is a formal demarcation, a way of stating, "Now I begin." In Tibet there is a whole language around demarcation and boundaries, such as "boundary stones" marking practice space, and other markings of physical and temporal boundaries to indicate, "Now I am engaging in this activity." The beginning moment is also a reflective moment in which one asks, "Why am I doing this?" This scripted moment considers motivations, values, and goals. In the middle, the phase we think of as the actual contemplation, such boundaries emphasize the concept "I will be absorbed in an integrated way in this activity." And then there is the conclusion, a formal way of saying, "Now I bring it to an end. Now I dismantle the boundary. Now I move back into these other domains of my life."

This concluding moment also allows one to take stock of the situation, to consider what happened, to ask: "What were the experiences I had? How do I want to bring these experiences into my life, with which I will now engage?"

"Contemplation may often be slow and quiet, but it can involve spontaneity and social dimensions, as in contemplating a form of art, or the rapid interactions within a group."

We often think that contemplation is *intentional.* While that is certainly an important aspect, we are led astray if it is our only definition. Contemplation may often be slow and quiet, but it can involve spontaneity and social dimensions, as in contemplating a form of art, or the rapid interactions within a group. This framework of a deliberate beginning, middle, and end can also be brought to bear on these types of spontaneous and social activities. Another important idea in defining contemplation is the recognition that we are a product of processes and practices. There are biological, cognitive, emotional, and aesthetic processes that constitute who we are. However, practices are also ubiquitous—we are all engaged in practices of many kinds throughout our lives. Many have been unconsciously imbibed through childhood—linguistic, emotional, physical, and social. Because we are largely unaware of those practices, we often think of them as natural processes. Recognizing our practices as practices is often spurred by an external catalyst, such as visiting another culture and realizing that what we had thought was natural is in fact a culturally specific practice.

Practices also display plasticity, a capacity for change. Recent research has overturned assumptions about characteristics we thought were fairly rigid in structure for adults. Scientists are discovering that the brain, body, and emotions have considerable plasticity—a capacity for us to participate and interact with our brain structure, health, wellbeing, emotions, or personality orientations. While there are limits to this malleability, human self-awareness can be trained to take advantage of it. Through reflexive awareness, we can recognize the processes and practices constituting who we are at any given moment, as well as their specific outcomes. We can cultivate a variety of practices that use concentration, breathing, postures, visualization, cultivation of emotions, and so forth to bring our taken-for-granted practices into the light of self-awareness. This is mindfulness: watching our emotions, thoughts, reactions to other people, and bodily sensations.

> "Through reflexive awareness, we can recognize the processes and practices constituting who we are at any given moment, as well as their specific outcomes. We can cultivate a variety of practices that use concentration, breathing, postures, visualization, cultivation of emotions, and so forth to bring our taken-for-granted practices into the light of self-awareness.."

Through this cultivation of self-awareness, we realize that we can change these states of affairs. When we bring self-awareness to our own processes and practices, they change in the moment—just as when we rage, and then bring attention to rage, and the anger suddenly changes in quality. Things that seemed impossible become possible as we recognize our capacity for transformation. Contemplative practice is trying to work in that space between the practices we engage in and our awareness of them.

Yet there are different modes of awareness. There is an awareness that focuses on noticing things, analytical awareness, aesthetic awareness, interpretive awareness, or narrative awareness. It takes many forms as we use it for different purposes and direct it to different types of objects. When we begin to cultivate awareness, we see that it is not neutral. Buddhist meditation, which involves meditating on objects, commonly teaches that meditating on different things requires different types of awareness. Depending on what our agenda is and what form of awareness we try to elicit, the meditation will have its specific impacts. While often we think of meditation as biased toward the mind and thoughts, a broader interpretation recognizes that the focus could be on the body, emotions, or social relationships; the common ingredient is the idea of different forms of awareness. In the Buddhist context, awareness does not have to be self-conscious, since many modes of awareness operate below the level of consciousness. Regardless of what is involved—the body, postures, breathing, visualizations, and so forth—contemplation always includes awareness on one level or another. It is about the training of awareness, the understanding of different forms of awareness, and, ultimately, the transformation of awareness.

The big question, then, is how do you train in contemplative awareness? What are its essential elements and framing contexts? Buddhist meditation involves breath, postures, visual components, analysis, and awareness. But we must also pause to consider the context. In the Buddhist context, meditation is not primarily about dealing with personal problems—coping with crisis, smoothing out relationships, or improving parenting. It is more about general human problems of suffering, exploitation, desire, attachment, a need for understanding. Buddhist meditation is first and foremost about "soteriology," or salvation. What we see today in American culture in mindfulness and marketing—where meditation is often about improving job productivity, sex life, parenting, relationships—is a significant change from a traditional religious context. When we look at secular contemplation or the mindfulness revolution, it becomes important to consider the values with which we are trying to align. Often, we are shocked to discover that the values we exemplify in our behavior differ significantly from the values with which we declaratively align. Contemplation is a way to both catch sight of the values that we communicate in our life and adjust our behavior at the instinctive level for full integration of values in our words and lives. We could call this "contemplative literacy," becoming literate in ourselves, our bodies, speech, mind.

Perhaps contemplation is thus most centrally about the nature and character of learning and its relationship to our own evolving self-understanding. With the new contemplative sciences initiatives, UVA has the opportunity to reimagine the possibilities of how our students, faculty, and staff can learn, and through such learning, articulate and sustain a better world at individual and collective levels.

The Phillips Collection

There came a time when sorrow all but overwhelmed me. Then I turned to my love of painting for the will to live.... At my period of crisis I was prompted to create something that would express my awareness to life's returning joys and my potential escape into the land of artist's dreams. I would create a Collection of pictures.... So in 1918 I incorporated the Phillips Memorial Gallery, first to occupy my mind with a large, constructive social purpose and then to create a Memorial worthy of the virile spirits of my lost leaders—my father...and my brother.... I saw a chance to create a beneficent force in the community where I live—a joy-giving, life-enhancing influence, assisting people to see beautifully as true artists see.

— Duncan Phillips

A Collection in the Making: A Survey of the Problems Involved in Collecting Pictures, Together with Brief Estimates of the Painters in the Phillips Memorial Gallery.
New York: E. Weyhe, 1926; 3-4.

The Museum as a Contemplative Space

by
Klaus Ottmann
Deputy Director for Curatorial and Academic Affairs, The Phillips Collection

In 1921, the year the American collector Duncan Phillips founded his museum in Washington, DC, the Austrian philosopher Ludwig Wittgenstein published his first and most important book, the *Tractatus Logico-Philosophicus,* one of the most extraordinary works written by a philosopher—a book that in the end declares itself and its propositions as "senseless":

> My propositions are elucidatory in this way: he who understands me finally recognizes them as senseless, when he has climbed out through them, on them, over them. (He must so to speak throw away the ladder, after he has climbed up on it.)[1]

It is perhaps the first philosophical self-help book. It encourages its readers to know when to abandon language and logic and instead trust their imagination. Wittgenstein compared his writing to "a mirror in which my reader can see his own thinking with all its deformities so that, helped in this way, he can put it right."[2]

Many years later, in a lecture on ethics, Wittgenstein announced from the outset that the topic of his lecture is really aesthetics: "I am going to use the term Ethics in a slightly wider sense, in a sense in fact which includes what I believe to be the most essential part of what is generally called Aesthetics."[3]

In a logic made up exclusively of statements of fact, ethics and religion are deterritorialized, oppressed, and, like beauty, beyond language. Thus Wittgenstein writes:

> My whole tendency and I believe the tendency of all men who ever tried to write or talk about Ethics or Religion was to run against the boundaries of language.[4]
>
> It is clear that ethics cannot be expressed. Ethics is transcendental. *Ethics and aesthetics are one.*[5]

Wittgenstein's words have to be read in the context of his understanding of philosophy (and art) as a *living practice.* Ethics includes an aesthetic component, and vice versa. For Wittgenstein, art and morality are closely tied. All aesthetic activity is also ethical, just as philosophy is a practice of life, or *Lebensphilosophie.*

Ultimately, for Wittgenstein, the existential questions defining the human condition, the "riddle of life," comprise an ethical-aesthetical riddle: "The solution of the riddle of life in space and time lies outside space and time."[6] This ethical-aesthetical riddle points to the ethical aspect of art, that which the philosopher Roland Barthes called "the responsibility of forms."[7]

The archetypal psychologist James Hillman argues that connecting aesthetics with ethics connects us "more profoundly with the cosmos itself":

> How does your own particular aesthetic response connect with the cosmos? To begin with, the Greek word *kosmos* is originally an aesthetic term; it does not mean vast and empty outer space through which sealed-up cosmonauts fly at great cost. It meant the right placement of things, fittingly, becomingly.... "Cosmos" means that all things are on display, show themselves, and are presented to the senses, which respond to them with feelings of like and dislike, approval and disapproval, and with a varied and differentiated judgment of their value. Thus your aesthetic responses are cosmological, not merely personal. They are signs that you are here and taking part in the entire world order, which is from the beginning set out as a pleasing aesthetic display. The world is first of all an aesthetic phenomenon before it is mathematical, logical, or theological. So the most basic reaction to being in the world is aesthetic. That word, *aisthesis,* goes back to a root that means "I breathe in," like sucking in the breath when struck by beauty or horror.
>
> ...Ethics alone is not enough to make a change in the world. Alone, ethics without aesthetics doesn't hold...beauty evokes love.[8]

And from love ensues care for the world and the other—a transcendental ethics that is not a modality of essence but rather an ethical imperative, a site of responsibility for others. In transcendental ethics, we are ordered toward the other.

Hillman refers to this ethical-aesthetical state, where the good and the beautiful come together to induce personal and societal wellness, with the Greek expression *kalos kagathos,* an expression composed of two adjectives, καλός ("beautiful," "noble") and ἀγαθός ("good," "virtuous"). The French philosopher Emmanuel Levinas called it "otherwise than being," a state where subjectivity substitutes itself for another: it becomes the other in the same. It is inspired by the other, existing through the other and for the other without the loss of one's original identity.[9]

This "otherwise than being" is evidence of the "soul's active participation in the world," as Hillman writes. Practiced on a communal level, an aesthetical response evokes love, which, as Spinoza has written, "feeds the mind wholly with joy.[1]"[10] It is an active joy that leads to ethical care, and thus to societal well-being.

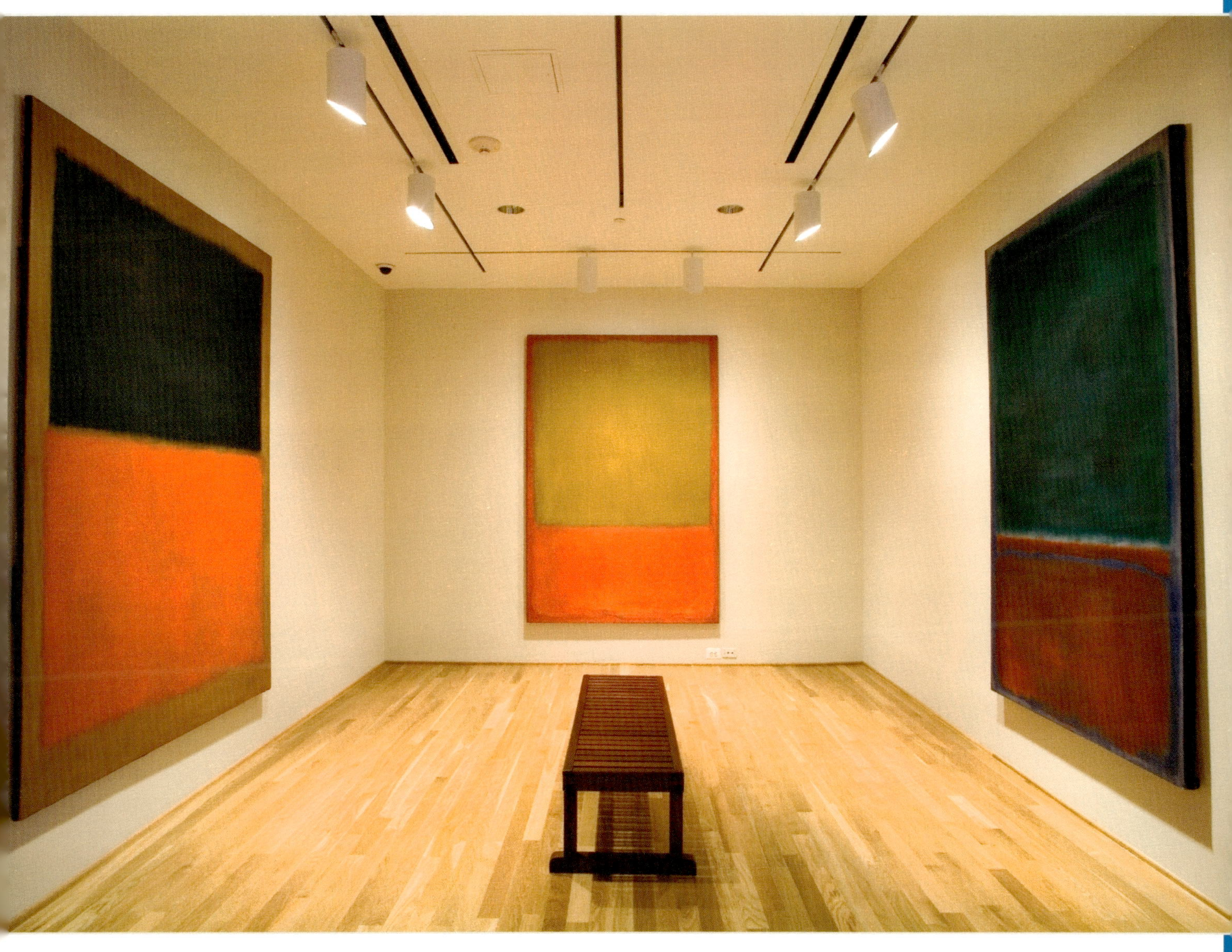

The Rothko Room at The Phillips Collection, Washington, DC

Photo © Robert Lautman

After painstakingly melting more than 400 pounds of wax, Laib used tools like a spatula and an electric heat gun to apply it to the walls and ceiling of a small chamber; he has said that entering a wax room is tantamount to being "in another world, maybe on another planet and in another body."

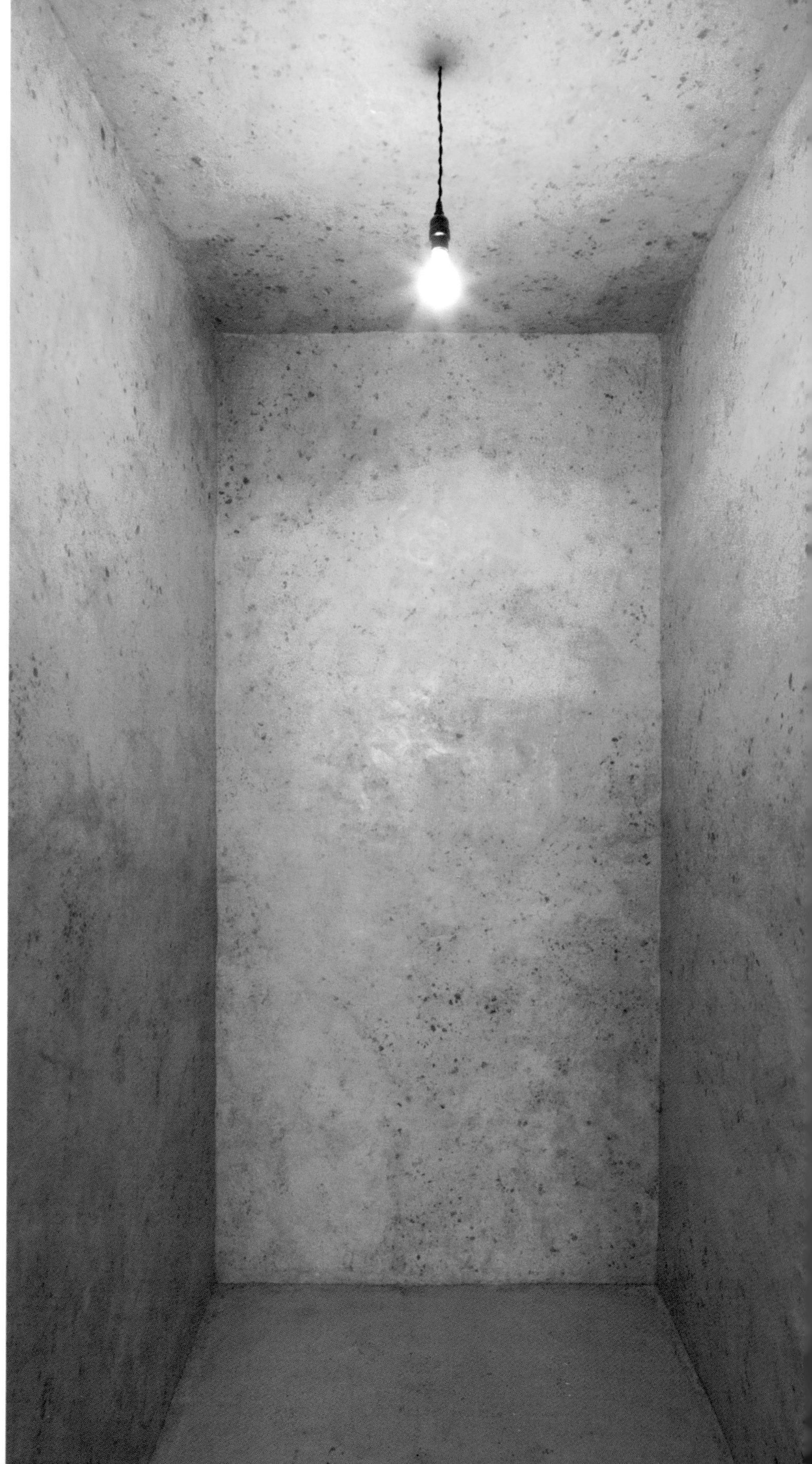

There is a deep connection between art, religion, and place. Ignatius of Loyola, the 16th-century founder of the Jesuit Order, expressed this bond with the term "composition of place." In his *Spiritual Exercises,* he wrote:

> It should be noted here that for contemplation or meditation about visible things, for example a contemplation on Christ...the "composition" will consist in seeing through the gaze of the imagination (*con la vista de la imaginación*) the material place where the object I want to contemplate is situated. By "material place" I mean for example a temple or a mountain...according to what I want to contemplate.[11]

Sacred spaces are where the soul, the spirit that presides over a community, dwells, continuously renews itself, and aspires toward holiness.

Sacred spaces are not limited to churches or synagogues dedicated to religious services, and most sacred spaces are characterized by an inherent minimalism that is expressed in the glorification of "poverty" as it is bound to the notion of a nonrepresentable. It is in this impoverishment that the aesthetic and the spiritual coincide, which is also the major drive toward abstraction in art.

For art to be experienced or observed, it has to be put in place, however temporarily. It needs to be *ensouled.* Without place, art appears to be "emptied of soul"—a mere commodity, out of place without ever being in place.

And for art to, in Hillman's words, "pull the heart's focus toward the object, out of ourselves, out of this human-centered insanity, toward wanting to keep the cosmos there for another spring and another morning,"[12] the viewer needs to be put in place as well and achieve a qualitative leap similar to Kierkegaard's leap of faith as "movement in place."[13] As Blaise Pascal once remarked, all the miseries of mankind can be explained by one simple trait: "Not knowing how to stand quietly in a room."[14]

opposite

Wolfgang Laib
German, b. 1950
Wax Room: Wohin bist Du gegangen—wohin gehst Du? (Where have you gone—where are you going?), 2013
Beeswax, light bulb

The Laib Wax Room is supported by The Phillips Collection Dreier Fund for Acquisitions; gifts in memory of trustee Caroline Macomber; Brian Dailey, and Paula Ballo Dailey; a community of online contributors; and a partial gift of the artist. Wax donated by Sperone Westwater, New York. The Phillips Collection, Washington, DC.

A highly contemplative space, The Phillips Collection's Rothko Room perfectly embodies Duncan Phillips's deep belief in the "life-enhancing influence" of art. Mark Rothko insisted on his largest canvases being installed "so that they must be first encountered at close quarters, so that the first experience is to be within the picture."[15] The intimate scale of the Rothko Room epitomizes Rothko's desire to have the viewer enter into the dramas of his paintings:

> The reason I paint large works...is precisely because I want to be very intimate and human.[16]

An intimately scaled and mutely lit space, The Phillips Collection's Rothko Room was originally composed of three paintings and referred to as the "Rothko Unit." Since 1966 four paintings, one on each of the walls, surround a simple wooden bench that was placed in the room at Rothko's request.

In 2013, carrying forth Duncan Phillips's belief in the importance of contemplative spaces in museums, The Phillips Collection commissioned the German artist Wolfgang Laib to create his first permanent museum installation: The Laib Wax Room.

In *The Birth of Tragedy,* the German philosopher Friedrich Nietzsche wrote:

> There is a need for a whole world of torment in order for the individual to produce the redemptive vision and to sit quietly in his rocking boat in mid-sea, absorbed in contemplation.

---

1 Wittgenstein, Ludwig. *Tractatus Logico-Philosophicus,* trans. C.K. Ogden. London: Routledge & Kegan Paul Ltd, 1981; 6.54.

2 Wittgenstein, Ludwig. *Culture and Value,* trans. P. Winch. Chicago: The University of Chicago Press, 1980; 18.

3 Wittgenstein, Ludwig. *Philosophical Occasions 1921–1951,* ed. James Klagge and Alfred Nordmann. Indianapolis and Cambridge: Hackett Publishing, 1993; 38.

4 Ibid; 44.

5 Wittgenstein, *Tractatus,* 6.421 (my italics).

6 Ibid; 6.4312.

7 Barthes, Roland. *The Responsibility of Forms: Critical Essays on Music, Art, and Representation,* trans. R. Howard. Berkeley: Univ. of California Press, 1991.

8 Hillman, James. *City & Soul, The Uniform Edition of the Writings of James Hillman* (vol. 2). Putnam, CT: Spring Publications, 2006; 153.

9 Levinas, Emmanuel. *Otherwise Than Being, Or Beyond Essence,* trans. Alphonso Lingis. Pittsburgh: Duquesne University Press, 1999.

10 Spinoza, Baruch. *Tractatus de Intellectus Emendatione,* 1.10

11 Ignatius of Loyola, *Spiritual Exercises, Exx.* 47

12 Hillman, op. cit.; 154.

13 Ottmann, Klaus. *The Genius Decision: The Extraordinary and the Postmodern Decision.* Thompson, CT: Spring Publications, 2015; 99 ("Kierkegaard's Special Individual").

14 Pascal, Blaise. *Pensées, in Œuvres complètes.* Paris: Gallimard, 2000; 583 [126] (my translation).

15 Breslin, J.E.B. *Mark Rothko: A Biography.* Chicago: The University of Chicago Press, 1993; 311 (Rothko quote).

16 Ibid., 280.

Contemplation Audio Tour
Can Looking at Art be Good for You?

by

Brooke Rosenblatt

Head of Public Engagement,

The Phillips Collection

The Phillips Collection's Contemplation Audio Tour encourages visitors to harness the restorative power of art. Drawing from meditation practices, the tour asks visitors to turn inward and pay attention to their senses, bodies, and breathing while experiencing some of the most celebrated works in the museum, including Pierre-Auguste Renoir's *Luncheon of the Boating Party,* the Rothko Room, Wolfgang Laib's Wax Room, and an artwork chosen by the viewer.

How does the audio tour combine looking at art with contemplative practices?[1] An excerpt from the Rothko Room stop, which focuses on the power of color, provides a snapshot of the experience. After visitors enter the small room, the audio guide invites them to pay attention to their breathing and release tension or stress. While exploring the environment, participants hear a new prompt every 30-60 seconds. These cues guide listeners to note their observations, physical and sensorial responses, and personal connections to the art. Example prompts from the Rothko Room include:

> *Choose a painting [in the room] that speaks to you in some way.*
> *Feel the painting in front of you.*
> *Sense where your gaze and attention are drawn.*
> *Explore the entire canvas.*
> *Sense the colors.*
> *Explore how the colors' depth and intensity vary throughout the canvas.*
> *Notice where you feel more movement.*
> *Notice where you feel more stillness.*
> *Look deeply, slowly, absorbing more and more.*
> *Continue to let your breath be soft and smooth.*
> *Draw your attention to an intersection where different areas of colors meet.*
> *Notice how this place of connection feels.*
> *Feel this intersection in your body or your breath.*
> *If you notice your mind wandering, just observe with kindness and return your awareness to your body and breath.*

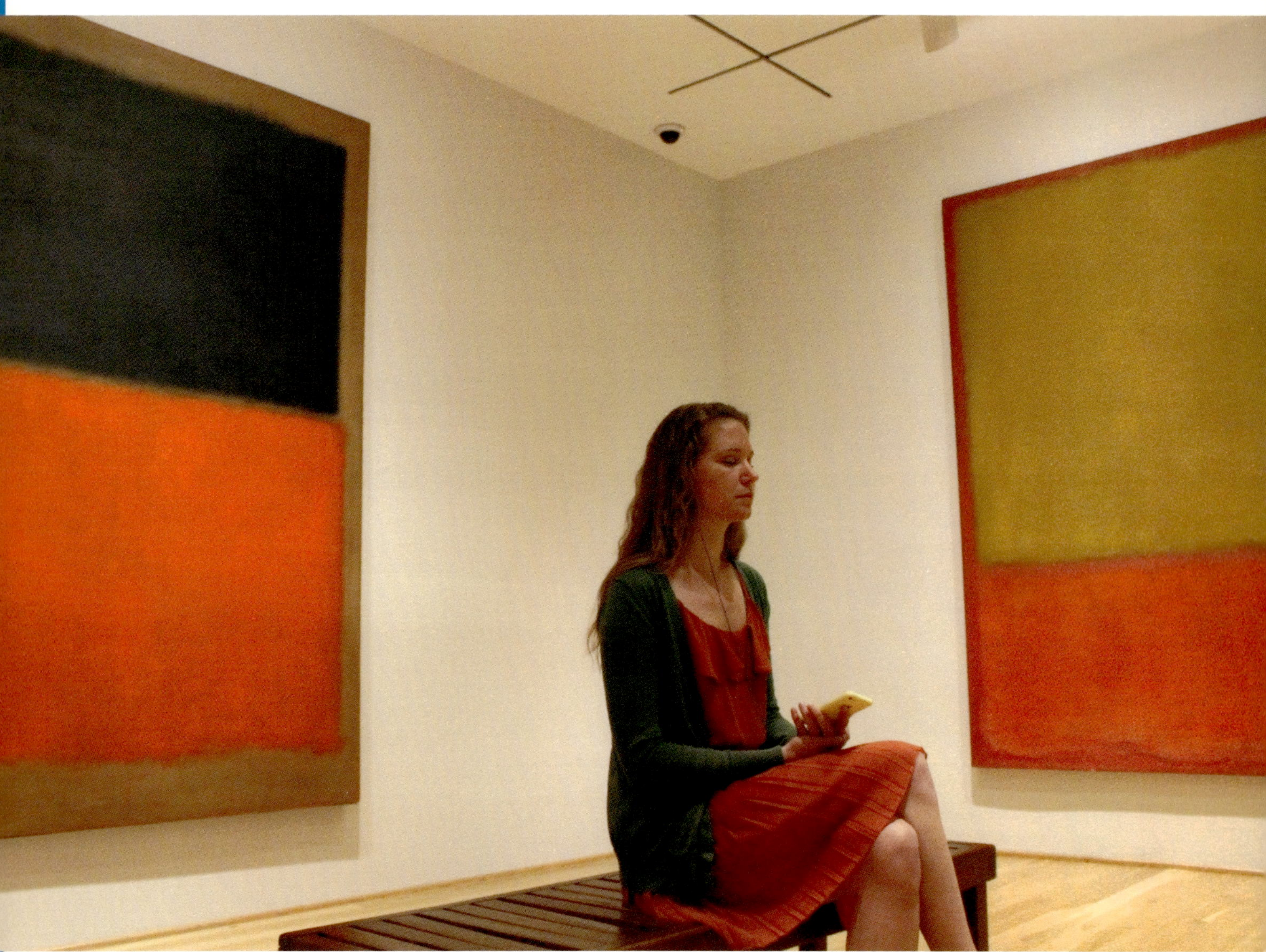

A visitor experiencing the Contemplation Audio Tour in the Rothko Room.

Photo: Vivian Djen

The tour continues by encouraging viewers to become absorbed by Rothko's fields of colors and to consider how the colors make them feel. This stop (and every stop on the Contemplation Audio Tour) concludes with personal reflection and an invitation to take aspects of the experience into the world beyond the museum. At the end of the Rothko Room encounter, the guide asks audiences to:

> *Become aware of the space around you.*
> *Feel this community of canvases.*
> *Absorb this room filled with color.*
> *Let this experience of slowing down and looking closely accompany you throughout the rest of your day. Be present with what you see.*
> *Pay attention to the world of color: tones, hues, and textures…the relationships of colors around you.*
> *Notice the incredible tapestry of colors in this world and in your daily life, and feel these colors nourish you in whatever ways you need.*

While a handful of museums offer programs connecting art with contemplation or meditation, the Phillips believes it is the first to translate this type of looking and contemplating experience into an audio tour available to the general public. Participants access the tour via cell phone, the museum's app, or a YouTube playlist.[2] Using a "bring your own device" model encourages participants to focus on the experience rather than the technology, which is pivotal when setting the stage for an unconventional experience with art.

Throughout the development of the Contemplation Audio Tour, The Phillips Collection collaborated with key organizations and professionals. The museum first sought input from the University of Virginia's OpenGrounds. OpenGrounds facilitated relationships with faculty and staff from UVA's Contemplative Sciences Center, Departments of Art and Music, and The Fralin Museum of Art.[3] These experts shared their knowledge on contemplative practices and provided feedback at various stages of the project. The Phillips also worked with local business Yoga District, and the collaborating yoga and mediation teacher lent her voice to the audio experience.

Before launching the Contemplation Audio Tour, The Phillips Collection prototyped the content and delivery. The museum invited yoga and meditation instructors, UVA and Georgetown University students and professors, and members of the public to provide feedback during live testing sessions. The museum refined each stop based on insights about what aspects of the tour might resonate with potential users. The Phillips also tested the cell phone delivery method. Some testers indicated fatigue from holding up their phones, and others found fellow visitors distracting. This feedback prompted The Phillips Collection to encourage users to wear headphones to focus their attention during the Contemplation Audio Tour experience.

Though the tour is relatively new, the Phillips has some preliminary data on its use and intends to conduct a formal evaluation in the coming year. Current research shows that the Contemplation Audio Tour stops typically have about 25–40 percent the number of unique users as the traditional art historical audio tour stops. This represents a small but significant portion of The Phillips Collection visitors who are interested in engaging with the collection in a new way. Participants usually listen to 4–6 minutes of each tour stop, extending dramatically the typical viewing time for artwork, which researchers situate at 15–30 seconds.[4] The Phillips has received positive anecdotal feedback about the Contemplation Audio Tour. One visitor commented, "Loved the Contemplation Audio opportunities, especially the Rothko Room." Another said, "I have never experienced this art in the same way. The experience was brilliant, please do more!"[5]

In April 2015 the American Alliance of Museums awarded The Phillips Collection's Contemplation Audio Tour with a Muse Award. These awards recognize galleries, libraries, archives, and museums for projects that use digital media to enhance visitor engagement, and the Contemplation Audio Tour was awarded bronze in the "audio tours and podcasts" category. One of the jurors stated, "With the advent of events such as Slow Art Day, there is a recognized desire to slow down the museum experience, and make it more contemplative. This audio tour does just that, encouraging deliberate interaction with art objects and slow looking. The high level of engagement and follow-through of those who take the tour is significant, and offers new ways into experiencing the art."[6]

The Contemplation Audio Tour is just one of the museum's art and wellness initiatives, and these programs resonate deeply with The Phillips Collection's mission. Museum founder Duncan

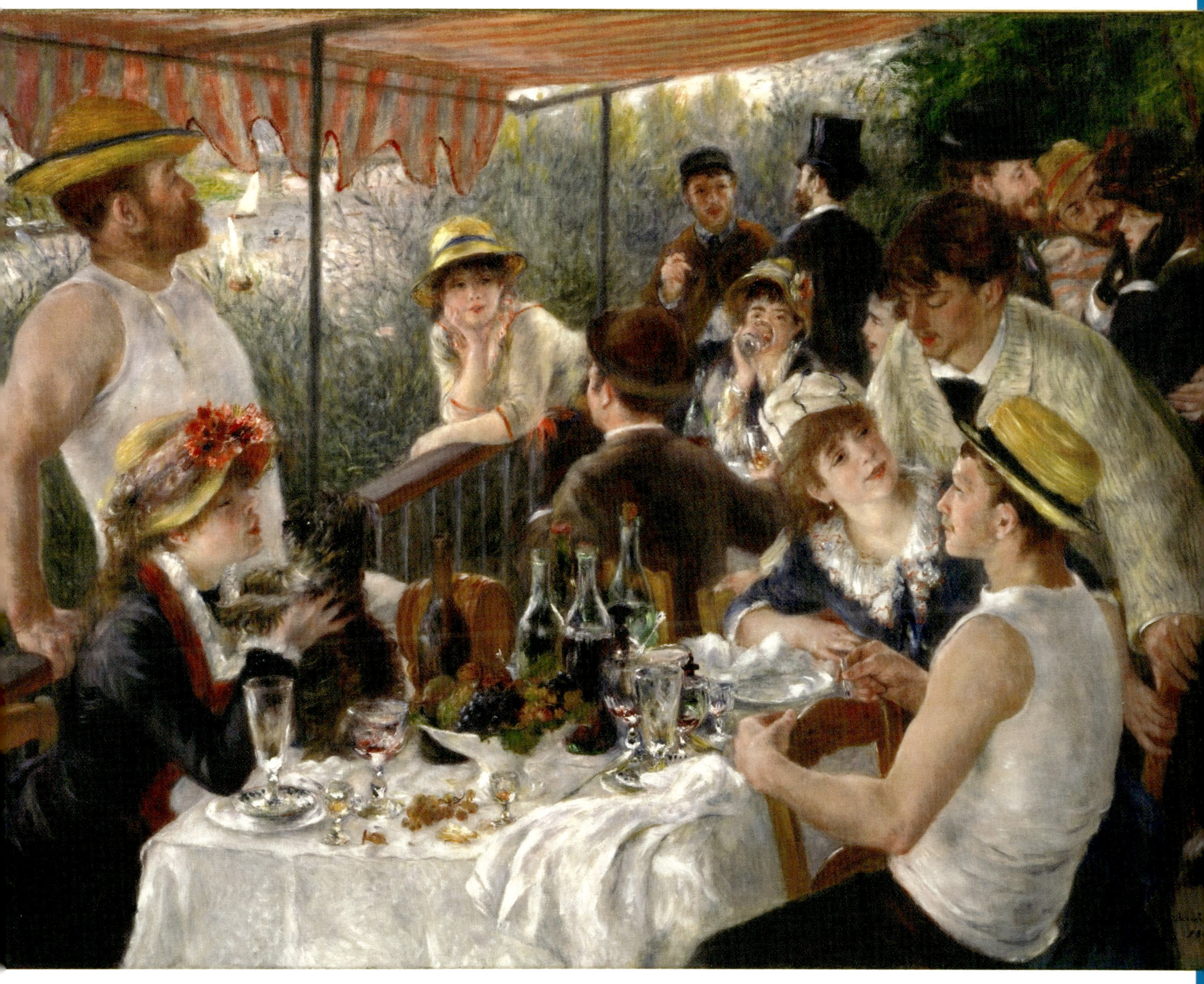

Pierre-Auguste Renoir
1841–1919, French
Luncheon of the Boating Party,
between 1880 and 1881
Oil on canvas, 51¼ x 69⅛ in,
130.2 x 175.6 cm

Acquired 1923. The Phillips Collection,
Washington, DC

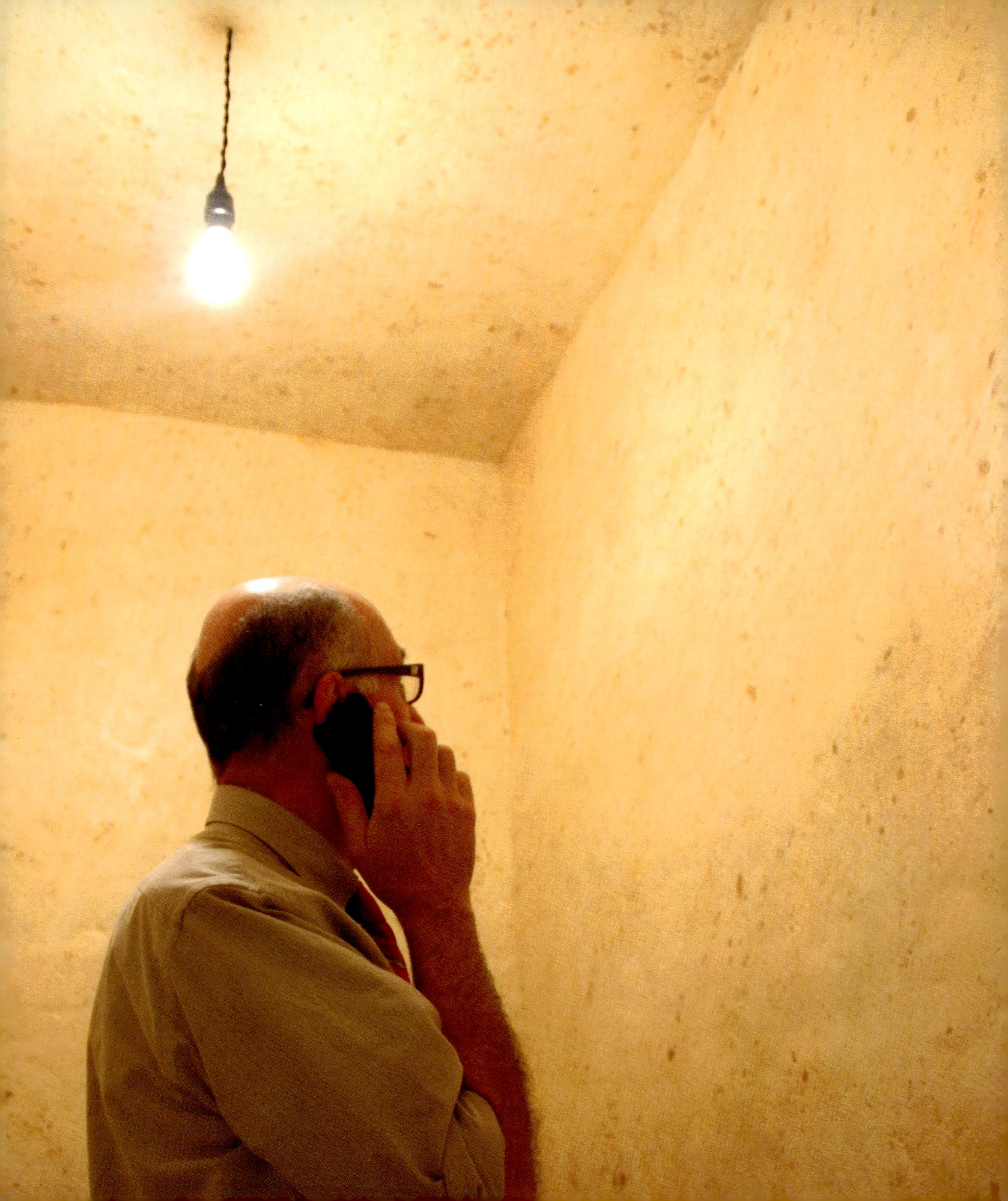

Phillips, after the sudden deaths of both his father and brother, turned to his love of art for consolation. Phillips recognized art's profound impact on his emotional state, and he wished to share its benefits with the public.[7] The Contemplation Audio Tour helps fulfill this vision by encouraging visitors to find new pathways for understanding and connecting with art.

1 Art historian and Professor Joanna Ziegler has explored the concept of contemplative looking, a practice she calls "beholding." Ziegler believed that attentive observation and consideration of physical and emotional responses to artworks helped her students engage more deeply and appreciate the artworks they studied. For more information on Ziegler and beholding see Daniel Barbezat and Mirabai Bush, *Contemplative Practices in Higher Education* (San Francisco: Jossey-Bass, 2014), 148-158.

2 The YouTube playlist allows audiences to access the full tour online. See "Contemplation Audio Tour Playlist," https://www.youtube.com/playlist?list=PLVAfcWzEA6ywsBp0L0bBQ4oBVJKn8XMkh (accessed August 6, 2015).

3 David Germano's insights on Buddhist meditation with a clear beginning, middle, and end provided The Phillips Collection with a useful framework for the Contemplation Audio Tour.

4 Rosenbloom, Stephanie. "The Art of Slowing Down in a Museum," *New York Times,* October 9, 2014, http://www.nytimes.com/2014/10/12/travel/the-art-of-slowing-down-in-a-museum.html?_r=2 (accessed August 6, 2015).

5 The Phillips Collection visitor comment forms, November 2014.

6 Stimler, Neil. "Muse Awards: Audio Tours and Podcasts," Speech, American Alliance of Museums Muse Awards, Atlanta, Georgia, April 26, 2015.

7 Phillips, Duncan. *The Introduction to the Collection in the Making.* Gaithersburg, MD: The Phillips Collection, 1999; 1-3.

opposite

A visitor experiencing the Contemplation Audio Tour in Wolfgang Laib's Wax Room.

Photo: Vivian Djen

Building Bridges across Knowledge Domains

by
JD Talasek
Director, Cultural Programs, National Academy of Sciences

What's in a label? The taxonomy of disciplines has contributed greatly in developing deep knowledge and expertise. The labels we put on categories of knowledge, such as art and science, have great cognitive power, facilitating understanding, learning, and communication. Naming and categorizing is, after all, how humans think. But these labels conjure assumptions and biases that might also raise barriers in the way we think or problem solve. The ideas and challenges of the 21st century do not often fit neatly into our constructed domains of knowledge. This need to meet new challenges is leading many who are focused on problem solving to look outside their own areas of expertise for inspiration, collaboration, and unique approaches to finding answers. Historically, after all, new ideas have seldom come from strictly following traditions and expected methodologies.

This desire to look beyond traditional areas of exploration at times seems to be fueled by better networking opportunities and the need for informal spaces of learning and collaboration—creating spaces, perhaps, where the "eureka moment" might live. But what if those with "deep" expertise could find more efficient ways of working together—to inform one another where the sum becomes greater than the parts? What would this type of space look like? What would the experience feel like?

The need to create a space where people working in the grey area between silos could meet, socialize, and network on a regular basis was the driving force behind the formation of DASER or DC Art Science Evening Rendezvous. Nearly once a month, DASER, organized by the Cultural Programs of the National Academy of Sciences (CPNAS), hosts presentations by scientists and artists in the region to engage in cross-disciplinary discussion. The hope is that this salon will increase familiarity across disciplines with the unique speech communities that have evolved and help break down other barriers that might prevent engagement outside of specialized territories.

Why do this? Even experts benefit from a new perspective. Over the past decade many universities, educational institutions, and cultural centers have explored ways of bringing practitioners from many disciplines together for further research and public engagement. DASER provides a place for these practitioners to reach outside of their institutions and to share and gain knowledge.

When DASER was established as part of CPNAS five years ago, the format was inspired by the LASER series (Leonardo Art Science Evening Rendezvous). This similar program, the brainchild of Pierro Scaruffi, was formed in 2008 in collaboration with Leonardo: International Society of Arts, Science and Technology, a network that has been actively building bridges between disciplines since the 1960s. Since that time, the need for these bridges has catalyzed many other LASER programs in cities including Los Angeles, New York, Santa Cruz, Toronto, and London. While these programs operate to reflect local activities between art and science, together they form a larger international network of activity. The expansion of these programs over the past five years and the increase in public attendance indicate a fundamental, growing interest in this form of engagement.

In the spirit of promoting cross-disciplinary interactions in our community, the February 2015 DASER focused on the outcomes of last year's annual Art and Innovation Conference, an ongoing collaboration between OpenGrounds at the University of Virginia and The Phillips Collection's Center for the Study of Modern Art in Washington, DC. The theme was art and wellness, and the DASER presentations in February provided an opportunity to share this work with a public audience.

The DASER evening began with a presentation by Fred Everett Maus, who taught a UVA seminar in 2014 on Music and Consciousness, in which students were encouraged to blend theory and experience. Among the topics of the course were music and meditation, music therapy, improvisation, and the innovative practices of John Cage and Fluxus.

Following Maus was a presentation on the cultivation of resiliency through contemplative drawing. Dorrie Fontaine and Barbara Bernstein discussed one of their programs, developed by the School of Nursing's Compassionate Care Initiative, where drawing exercises—designed to encourage contemplation—were aimed at improving concentration and sustaining attention while enriching self-awareness and confidence.

To add balance to the evening and reflect how the collaboration between the University of Virginia and The Phillips Collection has aimed to enrich the understanding and appreciation of art, Brooke Rosenblatt presented The Phillips Collection's new contemplation tour. Although a number of works at The Phillips Collection were specifically designed to be objects of contemplation and meditation, this audio tour experiment was created with the idea that any work of art has potential as a platform for contemplation.

The 2015 DASER evening concluded with a presentation by Marcia Day Childress and Jordan Love on Clinician's Eye—a joint project of the University's School of Medicine and The Fralin Museum of Art. Clinician's Eye is a workshop that uses visual art analysis to improve young physicians' core clinical observation and communication skills. Medical students venture from clinic to art gallery and are challenged by museum educators and medical professors to observe and articulate what they see in the art before them.

All four presentations (which are archived online on the CPNAS YouTube channel along with the past five years of DASER talks) represented conversations and outcomes from a collaboration that encouraged dialogue not only throughout campus but across institutions and into the public domain. Fostering connections between differing practices led to new and creative approaches both to health care and to art appreciation and education—the whole being greater than the sum of its parts. Programs were created that could impact training of health care providers...*and* tools were developed to aid in the appreciation of works of art. This is often a unique characteristic of cross-disciplinary collaboration and one that is frequently underappreciated and underdeveloped—the idea of multiple outcomes. Creating spaces where experts can inspire one another and develop new approaches to problem solving with a multiplicity of outcomes is an academic challenge for the 21st century.

Clinician's Eye

by

Marcia Day Childress PhD
Associate Professor of Medical Education (Medical Humanities)
Director of Programs in Humanities, Center for Biomedical Ethics and Humanities, University of Virginia School of Medicine

Jordan Love PhD
Academic Curator, The Fralin Museum of Art, University of Virginia

Clinician's Eye is a joint educational project of the University of Virginia's Fralin Museum of Art and the UVA School of Medicine's Center for Biomedical Ethics and Humanities. This highly interactive workshop is an exercise in mindful, deliberate attention that uses visual art analysis to help medical students and other health professionals improve their core clinical skills in observation, collaboration, communication, compassion, and reflection.

Developed in 2012–2013, Clinician's Eye takes cues from medical school and museum partnerships and from related research at several other leading medical schools, including Yale, Harvard, Cornell, Columbia, the University of Texas at San Antonio, and the University of Southern California.[1] But UVA's program is our own, designed in-house by Jordan Love, The Fralin Museum's academic curator, and piloted with a variety of medical student classes through the Center for Biomedical Ethics and Humanities. Since Fall 2014, as the result of a curriculum committee decision, Clinician's Eye has been a required part of every UVA medical student's education.

Clinician's Eye can take place in a classroom or auditorium, but our preferred venue is the art museum, in part because of its wealth and variety of art objects and in part because the gallery setting can be a refreshing change for health professionals, sharpening the mind and soothing the spirit. Every semester the museum's exhibitions turn over, which means that new artwork, including pieces on loan and some from the permanent collection, can be utilized in each workshop. As a set of activities, Clinician's Eye is sufficiently flexible to accommodate this changing subject matter. As a result, the workshop is always fresh and offers new perspectives to repeat attendees—not to mention the instructors!

Clinician's Eye can be conducted with large groups (or online, though we neither do nor recommend this), but we prefer to work with small groups of participants. A cluster of ten or so learners can move about the museum, convening for different parts of the workshop before different individual works of art. The immediacy, close interpersonal communication, and sharing of perspectives that happen when the cluster has a close encounter with a painting, photograph, or sculpture all seem to benefit the participants. The small-group setting also helps even the quietest students speak up and interact more freely and fully with their peers.

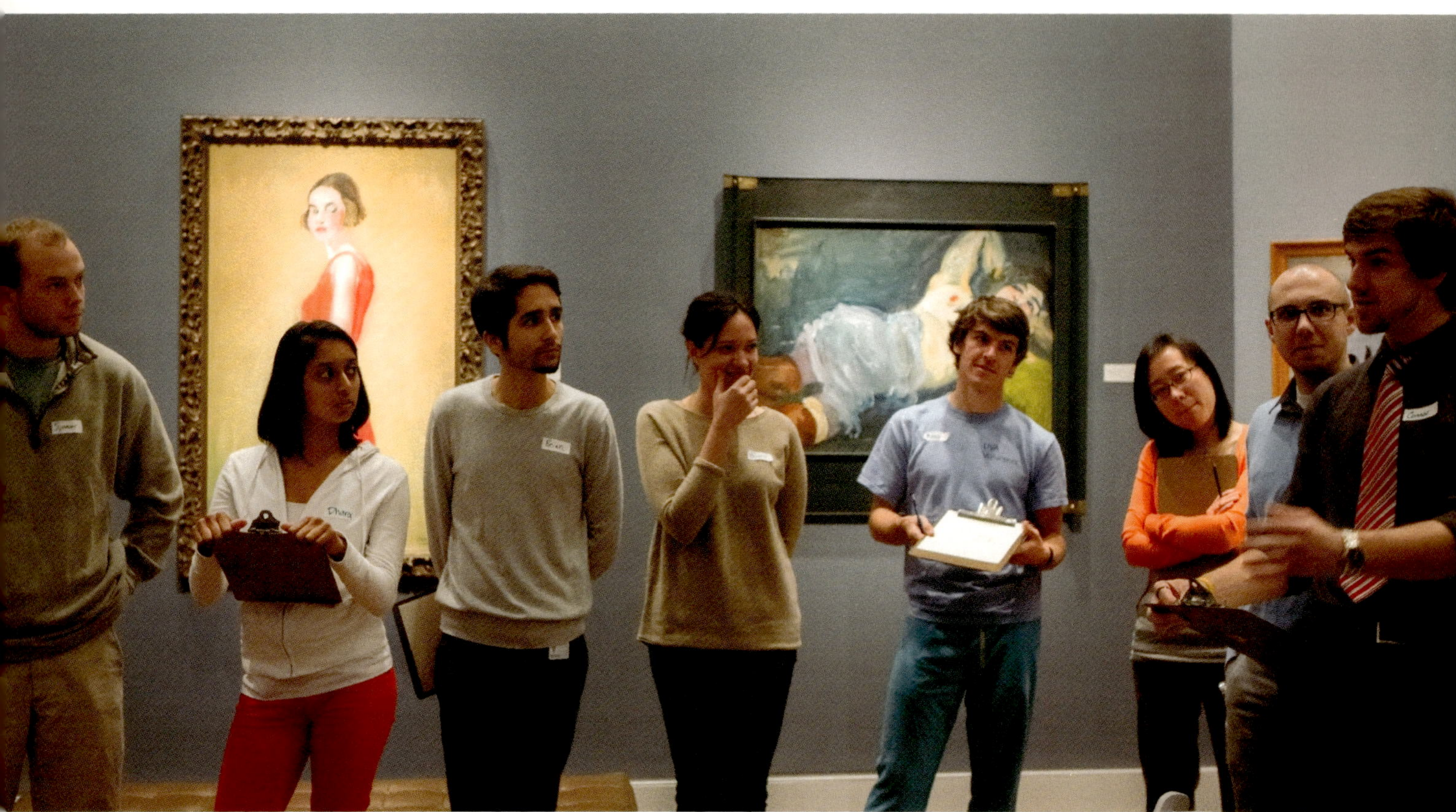

UVA medical students at
The Fralin Museum of Art

Photo: Stacey Evans

opposite

Emilie Charmy
1878–1974, French
Portrait, 1921 (the girl in the red dress)

Collection of Pamela K. and William A. Royall, Jr., Richmond VA

In the workshop—normally, a two-hour activity—participants are challenged by museum educators and medical professors to slow down their looking. They are asked to observe, inventory, and articulate in a nonjudgmental way what they actually see in the art before them, usually a mix of representational and nonrepresentational works in different media. Questions for the group are broad and open-ended: What do you see? What's going on here? What do you see in the artwork that prompts you to reach your conclusion? Exercises include the group taking time to "read" closely and generate an inventory of all that they see in a particular work. There is also a hands-on drawing/describing activity that learners undertake in pairs. Both give participants practice in mindful attention, in close reading, in description and interpretation (and noticing the difference between the two), and in communication. An exercise in which learners generate words or phrases about abstract art offers insight into their own and others' distinctive ways of seeing and responding.

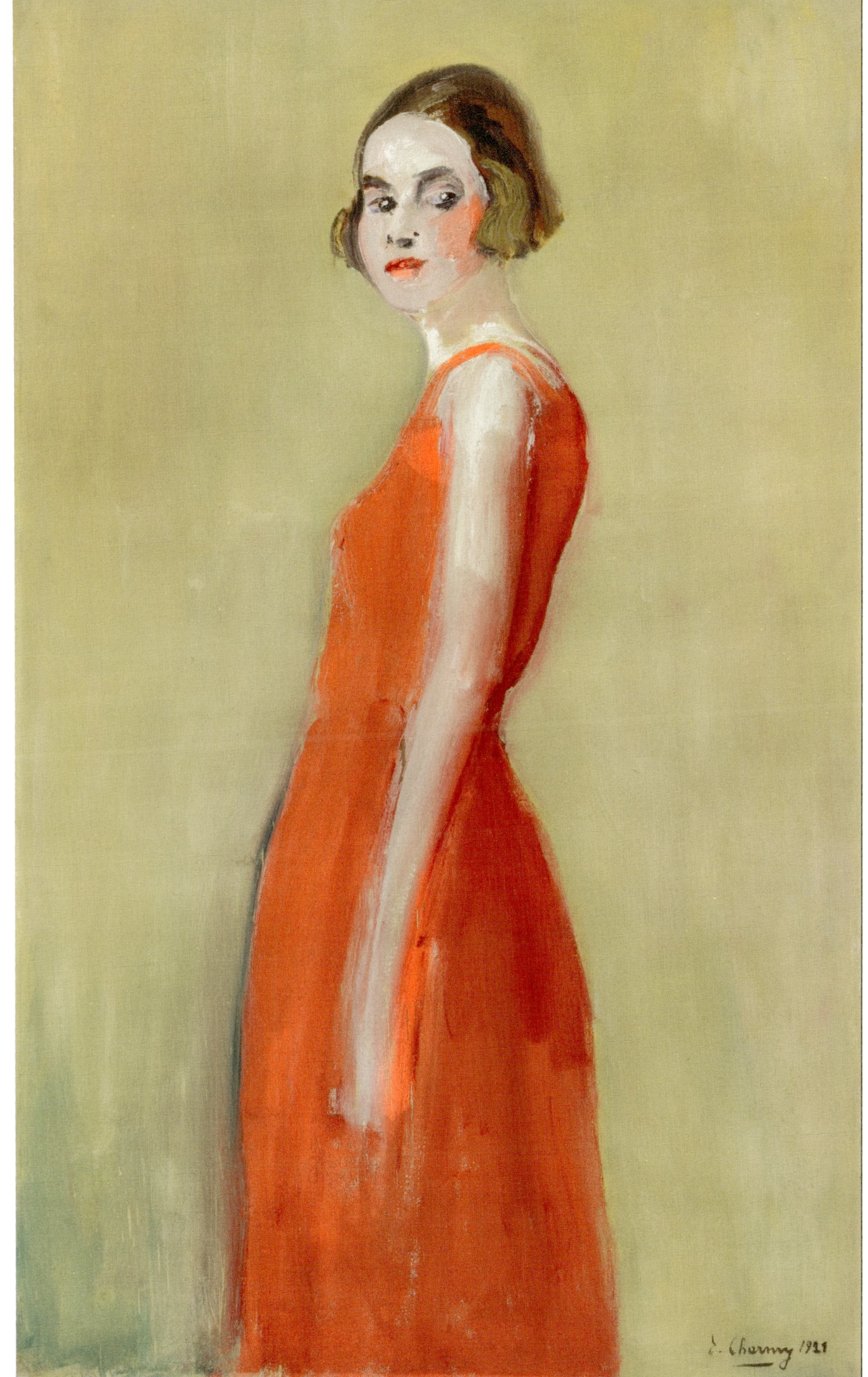

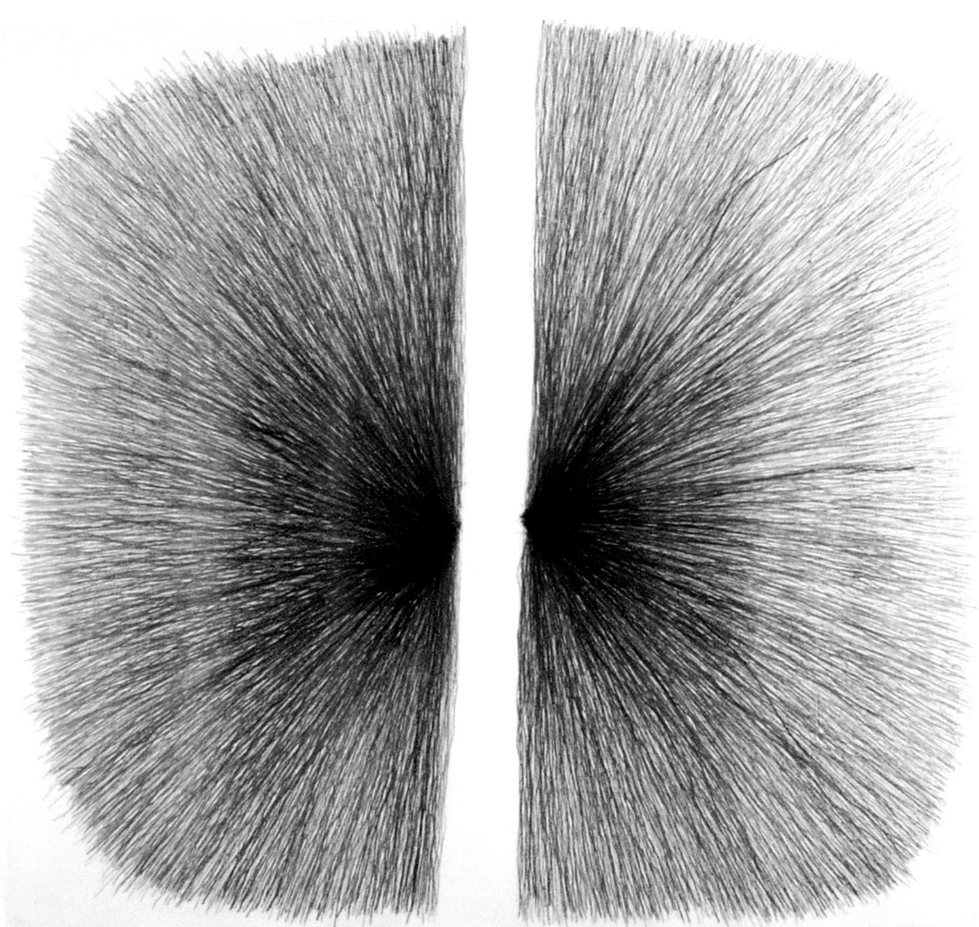

William Anastasi
American, b. 1933
Brio, 2004
Graphite on paper,
67 x 65 in, 170.18 x 165.1 cm

Gift of the Artist and Museum Purchase with Curriculum Support Funds, 2005.24
© William Anastasi

Clinician's Eye is designed to progressively stretch participants' comfort level with art and with their responses to it. The workshop starts with figural representations or works emphasizing realism, thus enabling learners to practice visual analysis first with recognizable imagery and forms of art with which they are somewhat familiar and comfortable. As the workshop progresses to the drawing/describing exercise, learners are exposed to ancient and non-Western art. The final, word-generating exercise requires them to engage with nonrepresentational art created within the past 50 years.

In all the exercises, we emphasize visual analysis over art-historical fact. Learners begin to recognize that art has multiple uses and that they need not be an expert in art history in order to use, appreciate, connect with, or find meaning in images they encounter, including abstract art for which overt meaning may be elusive. In helping participants acknowledge and accept ambiguity in the art they see, Clinician's Eye also helps them accept ambiguity elsewhere. For young clinicians who may crave certainty but whose practice is rife with its absence, these museum exercises may help them to accept situations that are ambiguous or uncertain. Indeed, when tested several days before and after a Clinician's Eye workshop, a small sample of UVA medical students demonstrated gains in their tolerance for ambiguity and uncertainty.[2]

The goals of Clinician's Eye are to engage and enhance learners' visual literacy, pattern-recognition ability, verbal and listening facilities, cultural openness and perspective, and tolerance for ambiguity and uncertainty. These skills, in turn, help build and refine the core clinical competencies of diagnostic acumen, communication, collaboration, compassion, self-awareness, and reflection—all capabilities that the good doctor should have. One clear benefit of Clinician's Eye is that, while it refines some key clinical competencies, it does so in a nonclinical setting, safely apart from the busy hospital environment and the demands of patient care. It also does so in the presence of art, which in its wholeness and beauty can delight, renew, absorb, transport, comfort, and inspire.

UVA medical students have responded enthusiastically to Clinician's Eye, finding the experience both educationally effective and enjoyable. And, while developed for medical students, the workshop works beautifully for clinicians of all stripes and seniority, whether doctors, nurses, or allied health professionals. We're discovering too that Clinician's Eye as a competency-refining activity translates well across professional boundaries, to students in the biomedical laboratory sciences, in engineering, and in graduate business school. A day at the museum may well be a wise prescription for any professional!

---

1 There is a growing body of literature about the uses and effectiveness of arts- and museum-based exercises in medical and health professional education. See especially the following reports: (a) Dolev JC, Friedlaender LK, Braverman IM. Use of fine art to enhance visual diagnostic skills. *JAMA* 2001; 286:1020-1021.(b) Bardes CL, Gillers D, Herman AE. Learning to look: Developing clinical observational skills at an art museum. *Med Educ* 2001; 35:1157–1161. (c) Reilly JM, Ring J, Duke L, et al. Visual thinking strategies: A new role for art in medical education. *Fam Med* 2005; 37:250-252. (d) Elder NC, Tobias B, Lucero-Criswell A, Goldenhar L. The art of observation: Impact of a family medicine and art museum partnership on student education. *Fam Med* 2006; 38:393-398. (e) Naghshineh S, Hafler JP, Miller AR, et al. Formal art observation training improves medical students' visual diagnostic skills. *J Gen Intern Med* 2008; 23:991-997. (f) CM Klugman, Peel J, Beckmann-Mendez D. Art Rounds: Teaching interprofessional students visual thinking strategies at one school. *Acad Med* 2011; 86.10:1266-1271. (g) Schaff PB, Isken S, Tager RM. From contemporary art to core clinical skills: Observation, interpretation, and meaning-making in a complex environment. *Acad Med* 2011; 86:1272-1276.

2 In academic year 2013–2014, 47 UVA medical students each attended one of three two-hour Clinician's Eye workshops in The Fralin Museum. Before the workshop, 37 participants took a pre-test that consisted of a modified Budner's Tolerance of Ambiguity test. After the workshop, these same participants completed the same Budner's test. Eighty-six percent (86%) made gains in their tolerance for ambiguity. Funded by an Ingrassia Family Echols Scholar Grant to Louisa C. F. Howard (class of 2014), this study was exempted by the Social and Behavioral Sciences Institutional Review Board.

Drawing Attention

by

Barbara Bernstein

Lecturer, Studio Art

"Drawing Attention" considers artistic practices as vehicles for contemplation. I introduced some of these strategies in a workshop at OpenGrounds, as part of the *Art, Contemplation, and Wellness* initiative. The OpenGrounds session incorporated brief and edited versions of a few of the methodologies I use in teaching a semester-long course.

These approaches have been helpful for those who feel creativity, in any of its many definitions and varied forms of expression, is intimidating or out of reach. The techniques have also been particularly useful for those under high stress, as a way to prevent burnout and alleviate anxiety. After only a few short exercises, there is improved concentration, reduced tension, and more stable self-confidence. Included in this essay are selections of students' drawings that are similar to those done in the workshop, along with examples of a semester's final drawings, representing the arc of the experience.

Initially and fundamentally, "Drawing Attention" is an inquiry into what contemplation *does,* not simply what it is. As in Zen koan practice and similar Buddhist understandings, the answer is demonstrated by personal awareness rather than by intellectualized, detached analysis. In other words, what does contemplation *in action* look like? How does it affect our perception of the world we live in and, more essentially, how we perceive *ourselves* in the world? The techniques used in the "Drawing Attention" workshop and in my classes offer an opportunity to promote an internal environment of clarity in perception, manifesting in an external result: a calm and fully engaged awareness that is alert and present.

Learning to draw is learning to see. When we think of attempting to draw, we generally consider the ability to duplicate a photographic representation of an external object or scene as the goal—for example, rendering a still life or landscape. "Drawing Attention," however, is about recognizing oneself, the ability to *re-present* oneself *to* oneself. This occurs without the debilitating apparatus of self-doubt or recrimination and by using the simplest of means: paper and pencil.

opposite

Figure 1

All images in this essay were produced by students in Barbara Bernstein's "Introduction to Drawing I" classes. None of the drawings featured here were produced by Studio Art major or minors.

It is important to note the temperament and ability that characterized the last drawing experience will be retained and sustained into the next drawing session. That is, if you stopped drawing because you were admonished and ridiculed by an art teacher at age seven,

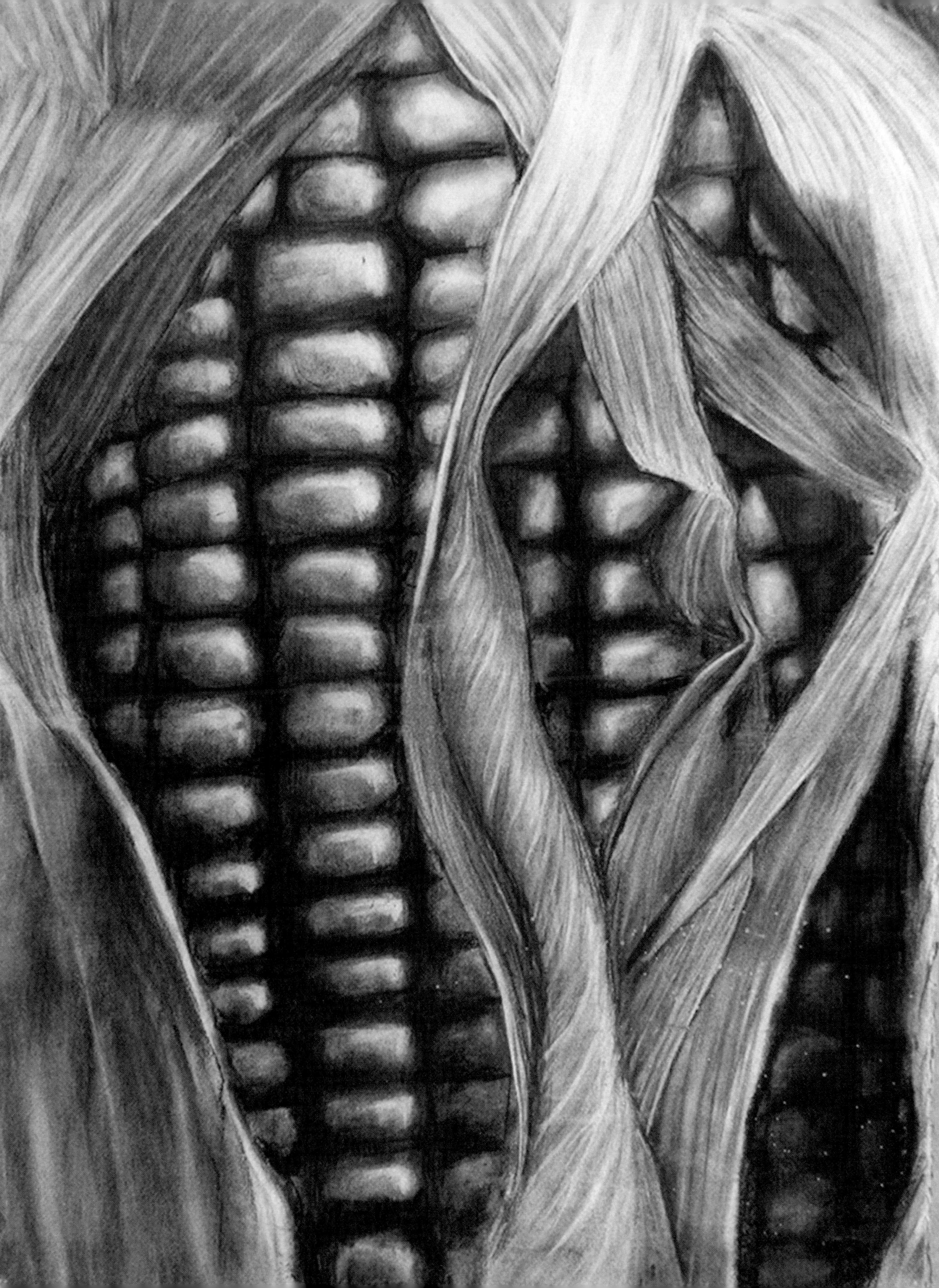

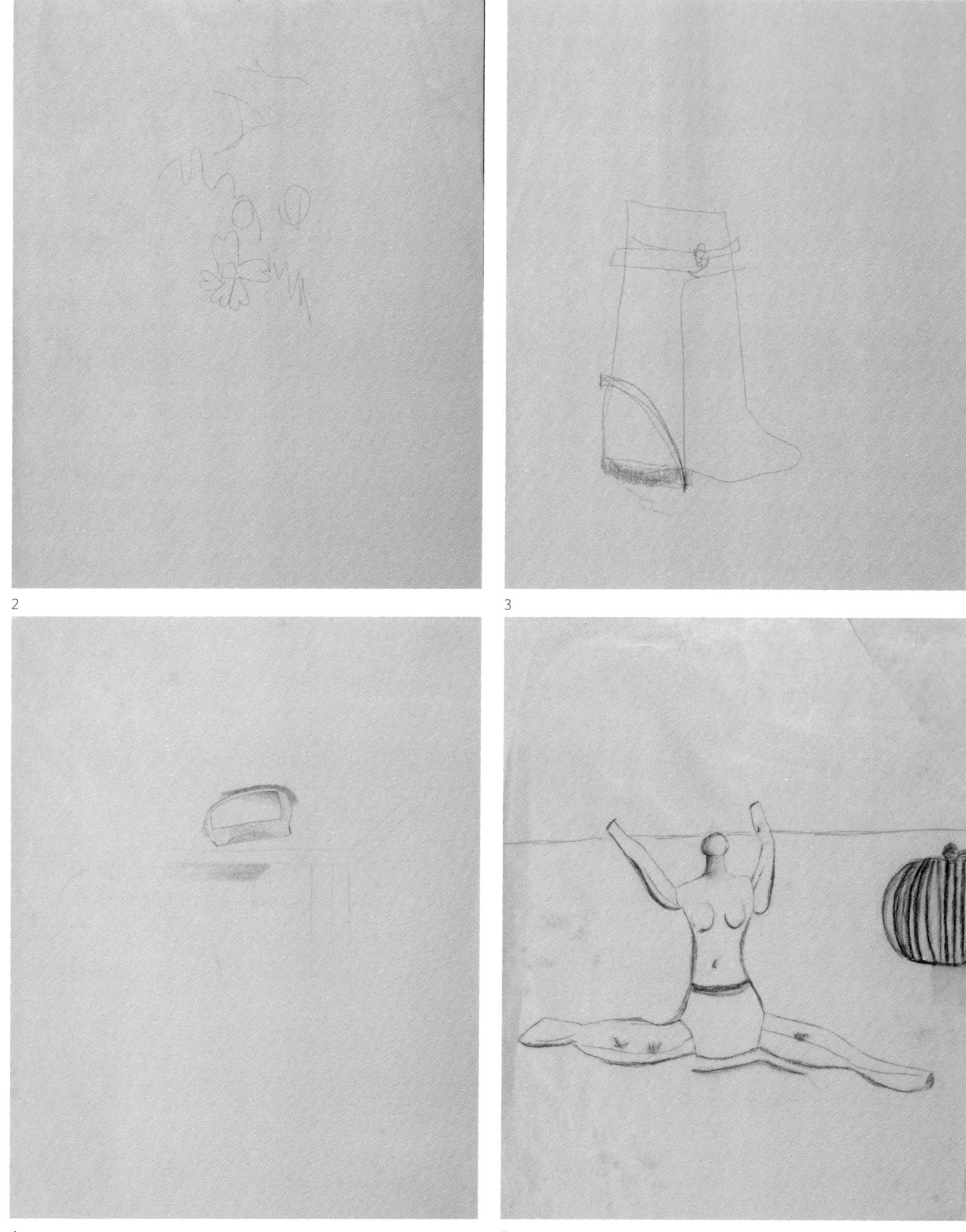

2

3

4

5

at age seventy you will begin drawing again as if you were seven. The way you hold a pencil, sit, breathe, and react to the paper and even the object to be drawn will be kinesthetically identical. "Drawing Attention" releases this imprint and therefore acts as a threshold and catalyst to be fully present, freeing participants to recognize where—and ultimately who—they are, without judgment. In the first drawings of the first day of class, or the first drawings of the workshop [Figures 2–5], the object drawn is usually small, out of proportion, isolated, and located in the center or slightly off-center of the page. There is a tentative approach in its rendering. The examples are visual metaphors of the participants' worldview and how they experience themselves in the world: unengaged, remote, and inaccessible.

In a typical class and workshop, the concentration level of the first day's exercise is approximately five minutes, occasionally less, but not more than seven minutes. The physical squirming is matched by a palpable lack of attentiveness and focus. As concentration develops, there is a marked, nearly geometric progression in the increase of confidence levels. Students and workshop attendees express how this is translated into their lives: their grades improve, new situations are not intimidating to them, they experience an assuredness in job interviews. Remarkably, even the unconscious habit to look at a cell phone is reduced! (In fact, the habitual behavior becomes conscious first and then the habit changes.)

As the drawing exercises progress, the question of "Is this right?" changes to "How am I seeing this?" This is a dramatic shift from the need for external approval and its attendant, debilitating criteria, to profound self-awareness, agency, and ownership. This newly discovered self (or, I would prefer to say, the uncovered and/or recovered self that was inherently present but hidden by doubt) overwhelmingly challenges and thereby alters the previous identity that was signified by lack, insufficiency, and defeat.

This heart/eye/hand coordination is an integral part of the contemplation equation. However, it is important also to note that this "contemplation in action" is not exclusively done using slow, unhurried movements. Drawing with attention (not tension) is the goal, regardless how fast or slow the hand is moving. It is, in fact, the eyes that control the velocity of the movement of pencil or pen. The slower the eyes crawl over the surface of an object, the slower the hand will move on the drawing paper. Likewise, when the eyes move quickly, the hand follows and the entire arm is engaged, moving rapidly. Gesture drawings are inclusive, commanding that the past, present, and future be seen and depicted all at once, similar to a gestalt-like experience.

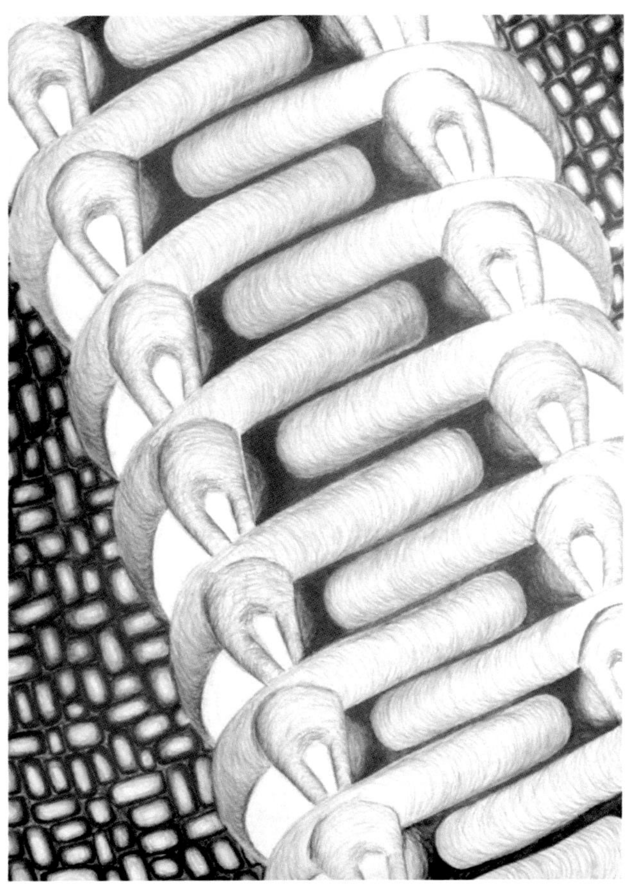

6

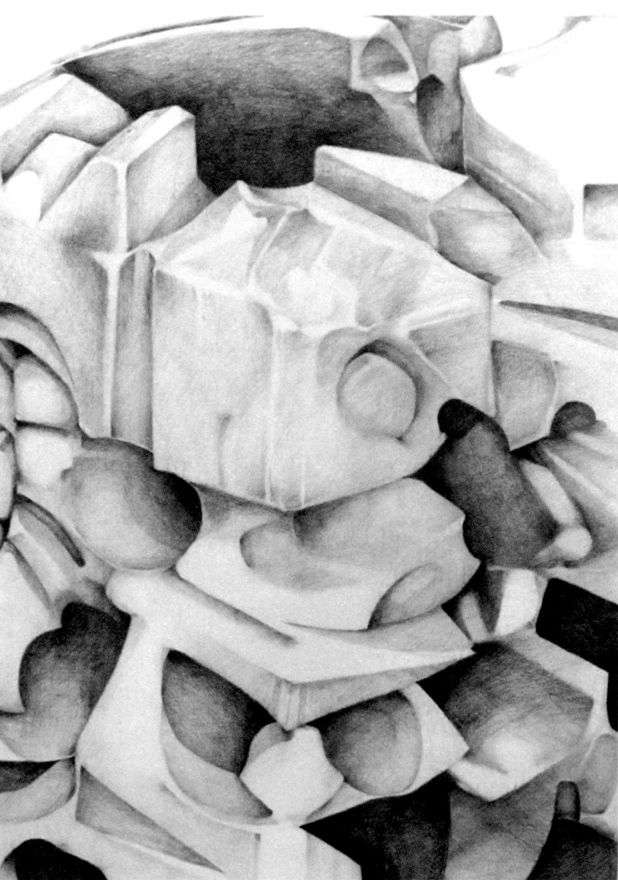

7

By the end of a semester, students who could not concentrate for more than five minutes are sitting for two and a half hours a week, twice a week, in total silence, without any interruptions, in total concentration of their work. They often comment they can't believe how long they have been drawing without taking breaks or even pausing! There is abundant verification that perceptual skills and drawing abilities have improved. More essential and sustaining is the transformation in their own attitudes about themselves and the effects of that change. Their *response-abilities* have significantly expanded; they are more open and accepting of themselves and others. Self-awareness, confidence, and compassion are the new personal equation; an integrated life has become possible. [Figures 1 and 6–9]

This essay began with an inquiry about locating oneself in the world through contemplative practices translated as artistic endeavors. Although I have made references to Eastern

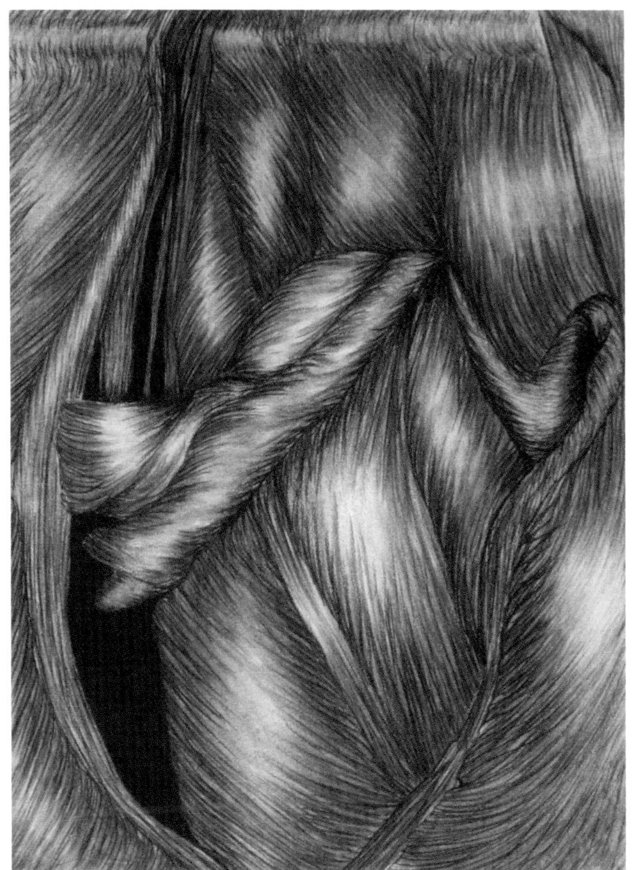

8

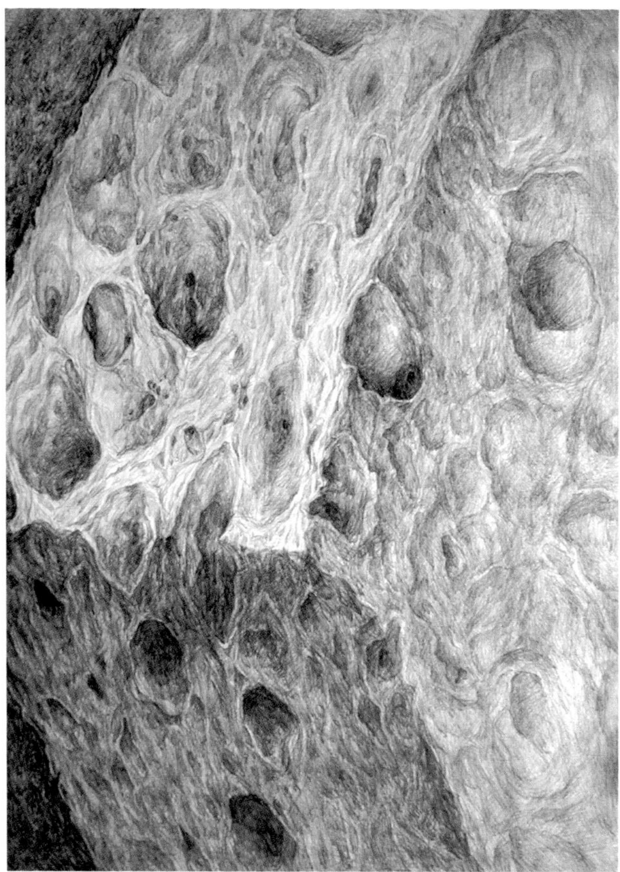

9

philosophies and religions, contemplative thoughtfulness is certainly not restricted to these mindsets. Many Christian, Muslim, and Native American sects among many others have equally pensive and reflective intents and objectives.

I am reminded of the first time God speaks in the Old Testament. The text indicates this is not uttered as a statement or proclamation but, perhaps surprisingly, is in the form of a question. God asks, "Adam, where are you?" At first we may perceive that God is confused or uncertain as to Adam's whereabouts. However, the question is pointedly directed toward Adam himself. God is perfectly aware of where Adam is; it is Adam who doesn't know. Tellingly, Adam is also unaware of *how* to find himself.

I believe that "Drawing Attention" answers the questions.

This is the kind of class that people will remember for the rest of their lives and that has the potential to change how we approach our everyday experience. Nothing is quite the same after this course, provided you let it affect you that way. I feel that I can better adapt to my life, and especially that I will never feel bored again if I can keep this with me.

— Anonymous end-of-semester student evaluation

music, consciousness, and healing

A Course on Music and Consciousness

by

Fred Everett Maus

Associate Professor,
Critical and Comparative Studies,
McIntire Department of Music,
University of Virginia

In Fall 2014, I taught a new course, "Music and Consciousness," an upper-level undergraduate seminar in the Department of Music. The course explored musical experience in a variety of contexts. Students read widely in interdisciplinary, professional-level resources, and we discussed the readings in class meetings. We also did extensive in-class experiential work and had wonderful guest presenters during the semester. The guests, funded by the Contemplative Sciences Center, included Stephen Nachmanovitch, an improviser and writer about improvisation; Sharon Beckman-Brindley, a meditation teacher; and music therapists Erin Johnson and Cara Marinucci.

We covered many different topics: personal interpretation of music; music and trance; bodily experience in relation to music perception and performance; the "vocabulary" of musical gestures in classical music; free improvisation; music therapy; Buddhism and meditative experience in relation to music; the experimental traditions of John Cage and Fluxus; and more. For the most part, our musical repertoire came from European traditions of classical music and from 20th-century experimental music.

The class met twice a week, with 75 minutes for each meeting. This is a good schedule for a course, especially if there are experiential components. Each class meeting has time for several different activities at a relaxed pace, but classes are not so long that they become tiring. Meeting twice a week gives good continuity from one meeting to the next. There were 16 students, a comfortable size for conversation and group activities.

I used techniques of mindfulness meditation frequently in the course. Often, we would begin a class meeting with about five minutes of meditation, which I would guide. I asked students to find a comfortable position in their chairs, relaxed and alert; I invited them to scan their bodies for tension, notice their feelings, and let go of tension when they could; I invited them to close their eyes, if this was comfortable, or to drop their gaze to the floor. Then I asked them to rest their attention on their breathing, as an object of present-moment awareness. I encouraged them to let go of any thoughts that came to their minds, gently, and return their attention to their breathing. All the instructions I just summarized are common in practices of mindfulness meditation (also called insight meditation or *vipassana* meditation), now familiar in many US settings.

For many people, mindfulness meditation is a valuable practice, with pervasive effects on other parts of their lives. I hoped to lead students to appreciate the practice, but I was also using it in the context of a music course, in relation to musical activities. Starting a class meeting with a brief meditation was helpful to students in clearing their minds, creating a boundary between their other activities and the upcoming class. At the end of the course, one of my students wrote this: "Because of our mindful practices that we would often start the class with, I will always try to shift mindsets when entering any classroom to be in the most mindful state as possible." Sometimes, to enhance the effect of moving into a special time and place for class, I would begin with a brief writing exercise, inviting students to jot down any concerns or preoccupations from other parts of their lives. In identifying their ongoing concerns and writing them down, students could set them aside for the time of the class. At these moments, and whenever I asked students to do in-class writing, I would write as well, following the same instructions.

Often we listened to music together in class. Music teachers frequently bring music examples into the classroom, but my approach in this course was unusual. I did not want to begin by asking students to "listen for" specific features of the music, as when a teacher asks a class to pay attention to the use of harmony, or instrumentation, or form. I wanted my students' initial experience of the music we studied to be open to varied personal responses. I would typically begin with a few minutes of mindfulness meditation, as a way for students to relax and clear their minds. Then I invited students to listen with eyes closed or looking down, to minimize visual distraction. After we listened, I would invite them to write about their experience for a few minutes, in journal-like entries that were only for themselves, not to be read by me or anyone else. I told them the goal of the writing was to sustain and articulate their listening experience. As I have mentioned, I would also do this writing. Then we would discuss the music together. Students told me repeatedly that their experiences, when we followed this procedure, were remarkably intense.

Sometimes I simply wanted students to encounter and explore their own responses to the music. Other times, the class would be on its way to discussion of specific analytical issues, but in those cases I felt it was appropriate for students to develop their own intuitive response to the music before beginning to analyze and interpret. This approach is consistent with my professional scholarly writing, where I understand analysis and interpretation as ways of clarifying and enhancing experience, rather than as distinct, non-experiential disciplines.

Early in the course, after one of our collective listening and writing experiences, a student told the group she was worried that she was not "doing it right." This saddened me, and reminded me of how often music education focuses on "correct" listening—noticing the "right things," not getting "distracted" by subjective associations. I replied that I didn't think there was any wrong way to be in the presence of music. Several students looked surprised. I don't think it was because they disagreed; rather, it was not what they expected to hear from a music teacher. I wanted to give students permission to pay attention to their actual experiences, whatever those might be, in part as a way of learning about themselves, in part as a way of connecting those experiences to the professional analytical and interpretive essays we studied together. In fact, we worked with sophisticated, challenging scholarly texts during the semester; students enjoyed them more and found them more valuable because we started from patient, unrestricted grounding in our own experiences. Partway through the course, in a paper about her changed sense of analysis, one student wrote: "Rather than seeing musical analysis as a disrespectful simplification of music into words, I now view it as a vital means for enriching music and proving its brilliance, depth, and limitless beauty."

Part of the course dealt with bodily experience in relation to music listening. To many people, it is clear that classical music somehow addresses listeners' embodiment, but writers and teachers often ignore this aspect of music. We worked with a groundbreaking book by music theorist Alexandra Pierce, who has studied, over many years, the use of bodily movement as a way of sharpening awareness of musical qualities. Sometimes her exercises seem simple—for instance, one can listen to music sitting down, eyes closed, and swaying freely, in whatever way seems comfortable. It is remarkable how such a simple exercise can heighten one's sense of connection to the music. After we explored this swaying in class, one of my students took the exercise into a choir rehearsal. Disappointed with a lackluster rendition of a beautiful song, "Shenandoah," he asked choir members to meditate briefly, and then they closed their eyes and swayed as they listened together to a recording of a sensitive performance. As this student wrote in a paper about the rehearsal, "I watched as the normally rigid members, with eyes closed and lost in their own worlds, began to embody the treasured song. They swayed with the song, becoming the river, and I could see on the faces of some that they were being physically moved by the piece." The rehearsal continued, and the choir immediately gave a much more beautiful performance of "Shenandoah."

Pierce has other, more specific exercises, such as following the curve of a melody with one's arm and hand, or replicating the "ping" and "lilt" of musical rhythm with hand movements. At best, these practices lead to a clearer awareness of one's embodied movement and, at the same time, awareness of certain musical qualities; the feel of the bodily movements becomes a nonverbal medium for thought about music, an alternative to verbal and symbolic tools of analysis. Before using Pierce's techniques in a class meeting, we often used meditation to relax and orient to our present-moment experiences. As preparation for bodily movement to music, we sometimes used a particular meditative technique, the body scan, in which one directs attention to the sensations of one's own body, moving successively from one part of the body to another.

Through open, contemplative listening and bodily movement, my students strengthened their relation to classical music. Then we brought our experiential, present-oriented approach to the 20th-century experimental music of John Cage and Pauline Oliveros, and the Cage-influenced art of the Fluxus group.

For instance, we performed several pieces by Oliveros (sometimes in my adaptations)—one called "Teach Yourself to Fly," in which meditative breathing led gradually to humming, then to singing long tones on each out-breath, and eventually back to silence; another in which students left the room, re-entering one by one, the students already in the room greeting each newcomer with a sound of their choice; and another where students spread out in the space of the room and then performed an action of their choice for each year of their life. Because the students already had experience with meditation, their ability to maintain an open, nonjudgmental attention to the present moment prepared them well for these pieces. We also performed a number of Fluxus events, in which simple, ordinary actions become objects of contemplation; for instance, in one piece by Yoko Ono, I lit a match and we watched it until it burned out.

We studied several uses of music in psychotherapy. We read about improvisation-based approaches, in which musical creation can give therapists and clients access to complex psychological states, as well as the listening-based approach pioneered by Helen Bonny. Now known as "the Bonny Method of Guided Imagery and Music" (GIM), This is a practice of individual therapy, undertaken by a client and therapist. In GIM, the people in these roles are called the traveler and the guide. The traveler lies down, eyes closed, and enters a relaxed state, often through techniques akin to mindfulness meditation. Then, listening to a carefully designed program of musical selections, typically classical music, the traveler spontaneously creates images and experiences in response to the music.

GIM makes use of a capacity that also exists, of course, outside music therapy: our ability to make associations to musical sound. GIM experiences vary in their qualities. They may be predominantly kinesthetic, or emotional; in many cases they are strongly visual, and may involve dream-like narratives with the traveler and other figures as characters. Sometimes emotionally intense memories come up. The guide repeatedly asks the traveler to describe what is happening, keeping the traveler engaged with the music and present-moment experience, but not directing the traveler's flow of impressions. If the traveler seems to be losing contact with the present moment, perhaps drifting into reminiscence, the guide may try to re-establish the sense of presentness, asking, for instance, "What is it like for you to remember that now?" The guide may also work to maintain the traveler's contact with the music; for example, if the traveler reports a strong feeling, the guide may say, "Let the music support you in that."

The goal of GIM is to give clients vivid experiences of their own thoughts and feelings. Within the environment of musical organization, and with the containing presence of an empathetic witness and the stable format of the GIM session, material often comes up that is difficult to access in other settings. The hope is that clients will be changed by having these experiences, especially across a series of meetings, and will also benefit from pondering the memories of the sessions. GIM is not like anything else, but there are affinities with Freud's procedure of free association, or Jung's practice of active imagination, or the use of Rorschach blots to evoke personal imagery. An important part of GIM is the client's willingness to relax and let content come up spontaneously, rather than trying to direct thoughts intentionally.

GIM interests me partly as a form of psychotherapy, using aesthetically beautiful material to create rich experiences and personal insight. But also, it interests me because I think our everyday, nonmedical experiences of classical music often work in similar ways. That is, I agree with music theorist Edward T. Cone that classical-music listeners typically give content to the events of classical compositions by drawing upon associations with personal experience. As Cone noted, such associations may not be fully conscious to listeners; the Bonny Method, however, encourages travelers to focus their attention on these personal responses. During and after the course, I explored these ideas at a professional level, drawing on Cone and other musicologists in relation to GIM, in a paper presented at the American Musicological Association annual meeting in 2014, and subsequently as a visiting lecturer at Temple, Northwestern, and Yale.

The relaxed, open listening that we did from the beginning of "Music and Consciousness" was akin to the experiences characteristic of GIM, and prepared us well for the study of GIM late in the semester. In thinking about GIM, students drew on a type of listening we had already explored extensively, and learned about its use in the pragmatic context of psychotherapy.

As I planned the course, and as we worked together during the semester, I knew that I was doing something different from my previous teaching. I had never committed so fully to experiential work in the classroom. I put careful thought into the design of in-class activities that would clarify the often challenging reading assignments. And I knew that I was using materials that could have powerful effects for my students—meditative and contemplative techniques, explorations of embodiment and fantasy, experimental artistic practices that challenge boundaries between art and life. I did not know how it would all work out. I was fortunate to have a group of gifted, open-minded, open-hearted students—though such good fortune is not rare at UVA. During the semester I felt that the students and I were flourishing together, and that we were sharing valuable explorations of music, play, pleasure, and meaning.

Still, I was gratified and surprised by the warmth of the end-of-semester evaluations. I have included some passages with this essay—partly to share my pleasure in the outcome of the course, but even more, to encourage other teachers who may wish to enhance the experiential qualities of their classroom.

A question on the evaluation form asked:

What were the most valuable features of this course?

Here are some responses.

- **Everything we studied we also interacted with at some capacity in class in a hands on or experiential way. It was an extremely thoughtfully crafted course and I absorbed so much information this way.**
- **Every class was [an] opportunity to practice what we were reading, to experience it. I wanted to go to each class—not because I was worried about attendance or discipline or falling behind—but because I might miss something phenomenal.**
- **The experiential aspect of the course was not only the most unique to this course but also the most valuable. I've never had a class that was at times so odd, and yet so focused on enhancing your experience with the material that if you felt odd about it, you were the weird one. I feel as if I learned more in class than I ever did in any of the books or readings, which I can't say for many classes, and the bleed through between class and life was incredible—truly a class that will stay with for me a long time.**
- **This course, by far more so than any other course I have taken, transcended outside the classroom walls and touched our lives in a very meaningful way.**
- **Fred Maus taught me to think about the world around me differently. I enjoyed his very open, low stress way of teaching. He taught topics because they were interesting and because he hoped to stimulate an interest in his students.**

The Fall semester of 2014 was exceptionally stressful for everyone in the UVA community. Above all, it was the semester that began with the disappearance of student Hannah Graham—we eventually learned that she was abducted and murdered—and ended, just before Thanksgiving, with the distressing *Rolling Stone* article about campus rape, singling out UVA for its central example. It was a semester of real heartbreak, and I am glad that, during that time, I was teaching a course that students found important and affirmative.

> "It is unlike anything I have experienced. I am not the same as I was at its start. I play music differently now. I listen to music differently. The objects and sounds in my living room now are not as they once were. I practice my music differently. I engage with my environment. I see obstacles as things to be explored, as potential sources of creativity rather than mere obstructions. Of course I can always improve, but I feel that I have been shown a direction that, if followed, will have a defining impact on my life as a musician, improviser, artist, student, listener, stander, walker, breather, human being."
>
> — Anonymous end-of-semester student evaluation

We had a class meeting on Monday after Thanksgiving break, our first meeting after the release of the *Rolling Stone* article. I wanted to mark our return to class, our presence to each other, as something special, and so we began with another performance of Oliveros's "Teach Yourself to Fly," hearing ourselves breathe, hum, and sing together. Later in that class meeting, we performed a piece by Fluxus artist Alison Knowles, "Shoes of Your Choice." In this piece, members of a group, one by one, place one of their shoes where everyone can see it; each one talks for a few minutes about the shoes they are wearing that day. Naturally, different people do this in different ways, serious or playful, informative or expressive... during the class we also talked about the heavy sorrow we all felt. On that troubled day, "Shoes of Your Choice" was a way for us to take pleasure in being together again. John Baugher, a member of the Contemplative Sciences staff, sat in on the class that day. He wrote to me afterward: "What a great day to be a guest visitor to class. Yes, the world is full of sorrow, and as we quake in the midst of that sorrow how joyful to allow ourselves to breathe together and to contemplate on stage the shoes that support us."

Early in the Spring 2015 semester, OpenGrounds hosted a forum as a celebratory close to the collaborative project *Art, Contemplation, and Wellness.* Given the topic of wellness, I invited two of my students who had written papers on music therapy to present their work at the forum.

— **Fred Everett Maus**, Associate Professor, Critical and Comparative Studies, McIntire Department of Music, University of Virginia

. . . . .

Music Heals

by

Katie Somers

Class of 2015

American Studies (Popular and Visual Culture Concentration), Music

College of Arts and Sciences

In Professor Maus's class, we frequently discuss music therapy and its function as a healing mechanism for people around the world. Until recently, I only understood this idea in the abstract. Few times in my life have I engaged in transcendent and healing musical experiences that have lifted me up and aided my own curative process; one of those times was last week. I debated whether or not to write about my personal experiences with this subject matter, but I came to feel it was appropriate given the recent events in our community. Ultimately, I decided to write about my experience to continue my own healing process. I felt it was important and necessary to write about music's healing qualities because I experienced the restorative and curative powers of music, and I believe others in our community will find their own peace through music as well.

The events of this semester have left many in our community, like myself, heartbroken and scared. Many students feel helpless and mourn the loss and the ugliness. I found myself reflecting on our studies of music therapy—about the articles we read, the case studies we looked at, and our class discussions. When the bad news came out, I immediately thought of our class when I contemplated how we as a school would begin to recover and how we could heal our wounds as a community. It soon became clear how I could help others heal and heal myself in the process: music.

Serendipitously, I had University Singers rehearsal not long after the news broke. At our rehearsal, I could feel the sadness and grief amongst my peers. A collective melancholy seemed to have washed over us all at once. Despite our sadness and disbelief, we carried on. We sang, talked, and went about our normal routine. Meanwhile, my heart was breaking for my school. I could not focus on anything but the sadness. Feeling broken inside, I found it difficult to enjoy my music or even to see it on the page. I left rehearsal even more upset and heartbroken.

Looking back, I saw that music did help me through this first day, despite my sadness. At this point in my grieving process, music forced me to acknowledge my emotions and be present with them. Thinking back to class, I remembered an essential aspect of music therapy: the acknowledgement and embrace of emotion as a part of the healing process. The act of singing, however difficult, gave me the opportunity to confront and accept my feelings. The music opened and prepared me for its healing work. While not obvious to me at the time, I came to realize how singing helped me confront my emotions. It gave me the starting point for channeling my feelings into something beautiful and restorative.

Another pivotal point in my healing process came the next evening at dress rehearsal. I had begun to cry while rehearsing "Do You Hear the People Sing" from the musical *Les Misérables,* and I noticed other members of the group crying as well. Tearing up, I tried to avoid the eyes of my conductor, until I realized I did not need to feel embarrassed for my tears because I finally had a sense of solidarity and strength. The choir's voices began to lift away the pain; something about our singing a song of freedom and courage gave me the relief I so desperately craved. I wiped tears from my eyes and smiled for the first time that week. I felt moved and empowered, and able to trust in my healing process.

At the end of rehearsal, I reminded everyone to get rest, memorize their music, and publicize the concert. Suddenly I paused and thought about what I had just experienced through our singing. I decided to tell my fellow singers about my feelings during rehearsal and acknowledge the grief most of us shared. I asked them to consider the enormous responsibility we had: to perform our concert to the best of our abilities so we could begin to heal and help our audience heal too. I asked the choir to embrace the opportunity to cast out darkness with the beauty of music.

During our concert, I invited the audience to engage with their own healing, expressing my hope that our music would give them restoration and peace. Throughout the evening, I sensed something special happening. The strength and love in the voices of my peers gave me joy and elation at being able to create beauty for someone else's benefit. By helping to heal others, we could begin healing ourselves. Looking back, I believe I experienced a form of music therapy through this discovery that music *is* therapy.

Our concert helped me find the beauty in the healing process and the light in the darkness. Music's restorative properties gave performers and listeners alike a chance to heal one another. Over the course of this class, a major theme has revolved around the idea that music contains therapeutic properties that help humans confront their emotions. My concert experience showed me that these properties enable us to engage in a beautiful cycle of healing and being healed, reminding us of the importance of music in our lives. I hope that through the current darkness we can find the light again in music.

Self-Healing with Music Therapy

by
Rachel Kim
Class of 2015
Music, College of Arts and Sciences

Since I seldom imagine music apart from performance and educational settings like concert halls and classrooms, the second phase of the seminar "Music and Consciousness" was especially enlightening for me. Each class took me into unexplored territory; this was particularly true during our extended discussion of music therapy. I had anticipated an impersonal survey of this unfamiliar practice, but instead I gained a deeper understanding of its varying procedures and also a greater awe of the human potential for creativity. I was especially intrigued by the functionality of music in therapy. While I had expected the systematization of music to demean creativity, I found that music therapy achieved the opposite effect: it enabled patients to self-heal by awakening a latent creativity that overcame life-impeding traumas and insecurities.

I had entered my seminar with an assumptive and uninformed perspective, due to my limited exposure to music therapy. Even the practice's name encouraged me to subconsciously overemphasize the therapist's role while failing to acknowledge the importance of the patient. I saw the dynamic between music therapists and their patients in the same way that I viewed surgery, with therapists "operating" on submissive patients. Tangled up in that medical association, I narrowly perceived music therapy as an artistic variation of rehabilitation: when helpless patients sought relief, therapists simply prescribed music as their choice of remedy.

After learning the basics of music therapy, I was fascinated by the effective cross between music and medicine. However, this systematic procedure of therapists treating their patients with music was unsettling for me. I had always admired music for its abiity to stay separate from functionality; its orientation toward creativity and aesthetics made it distinctive. But in the context of therapy, music seemed to be for use, manipulated for the sake of medicine.

With time, my perspective began to shift. Reading the various cases and interacting with our guest lecturers in class helped me begin to reformulate how I perceived the roles of therapist and patient, and thus uncover a beautiful marriage between science and art. I realized that though vital to the healing process, the therapists were not capable of forcing their patients to heal through music. And the mere sound of music was not a magical cure but rather the catalyst for positive change within the cooperative patients.

In medical contexts, patients may often appear helpless and dependent on professional care. However, patients in music therapy balance their dependence on the therapist for guidance with their own important responsibility to respond to the music. As they react to and interact with music, patients actively participate in, and even pioneer, the recovery process. In *Receptive Methods in Music Therapy,* for example, Denise Grocke and TonyWigram described how therapists used music "to evoke and support imaginal processes or inner experiences" in their patients. Although I initially overlooked this simple statement, I later noticed the patients' autonomy and creativity within the process. While therapists provide music and facilitation, patients imagine and summon their own visualizations. Creativity is often reduced to tangible productions and compositions, but this therapeutic process is undoubtedly contingent upon the patient's creativity, even though there is no artistic production per se. Music evokes and supports the internally existent, be it a memory from the past, an image of nature, or another creative response. After a therapeutic session of music and verbal guidance, the subsequent step is not immediate healing but rather a response from the patients. In essence, the therapists do not heal so much as they breathe life into the patients' latent creative reserves.

Consequently, I began to admire the therapy patients, particularly those in the case readings. To me, they were unsung artists who made music therapy stand out from other rehabilitation processes. Beyond their triumphant recoveries, they enriched my view of humanity through their candidness and humility. These patients articulated vivid visions, recollections, and images; their subconscious insights were surely more imaginative than they realized, which in itself exudes meekness and beauty. This posture of self-forgetfulness also appeared during our in-class meditation exercises. In post-meditation discussions, my peers expressed radically imaginative responses. From dynamic visions to out-of-body experiences, each person exhibited immense creativity, and I enjoyed seeing my peers surprised and excited to discover the extent of their artistic potential.

At first glance, music therapy appeared to be a simple and artistic spin on traditional therapy. But by embracing the entire process and not focusing only on results, I found that music therapy radiated an incomparable beauty. Combining music and therapy did not merely achieve healing; it also created a fresh and synergistic experience. As therapists invited music to speak into the ineffability of their patients' pains and insecurities, creativity burst through the patients' subconscious. And with the autonomy to respond, the patients demonstrated extreme power in their vulnerability—a creative strength born of a self-inspired peace with the past and confidence in the future.

A New Way of Seeing
Contemplation and Art

by
Naomi Worth
PhD Candidate, Religious Studies, University of Virginia

Art was formative in the establishment of the Buddhist nation of Tibet. In the seventh century, when King Songzen Gampo was uniting disparate Tibetan territories as a nation for the first time, he demanded that China send him a princess as one of his wives. He was so insistent on this act of deference toward the Tibetans by the Chinese that he fought several battles over the matter until, finally triumphant, he received Princess Wencheng from the Chinese. As her dowry, she brought a statue of the Indian Buddha Shakyamuni, called the Jowo by Tibetans, which sat on display in a temple in Lhasa for 1,200 years during the reign of Buddhism in Tibet.

Another of the king's wives, Princess Bhrikuti of Nepal, also brought Buddhist art as her dowry. According to legend, a tree in Nepal had spontaneously grown a Buddha statue. This small wooden Buddha was then encased in ceramic and placed in the Ramoche Temple outside of Lhasa, a structure built for his wives by the love-struck King. When the army of the People's Republic of China destroyed the Ramoche Temple in 1959, the inner wooden statue was smuggled out of Tibet and brought to the Dalai Lama in India, who has it to this day, continuing the deeply symbolic tradition art has held in Tibet.[1]

Tibet's art is primarily based on the spirituality of Buddhism. These pivotal acts in the founding of the nation of Tibet placed art as central to the contemplative life of personal transformation that developed and thrived there. The Tibetan tradition is known for its intricate and complex religious art, replete with paintings and statues of Buddhas, deities, rainbows, and holy beings. These images are not meant as mere decorations; over the years, each aspect of Tibetan artwork took on meaning that refers back to Buddhist teachings. For example, when trained Buddhists see the bodhisattva Manjushri (a common figure; see p. 54) holding a sword, they know the sword symbolizes cutting through deluded ways of seeing reality.[2] This is a common theme found in Buddhism—that we are mistaken in what we quite literally see, and also in how we view the world. With so much philosophical and practical emphasis on view, worldview, perception, and seeing, it makes sense that visual art is frequently used as a contemplative tool. Tibetan art is meant to be studied and contemplated; ultimately, its truth is realized in the meditation process.

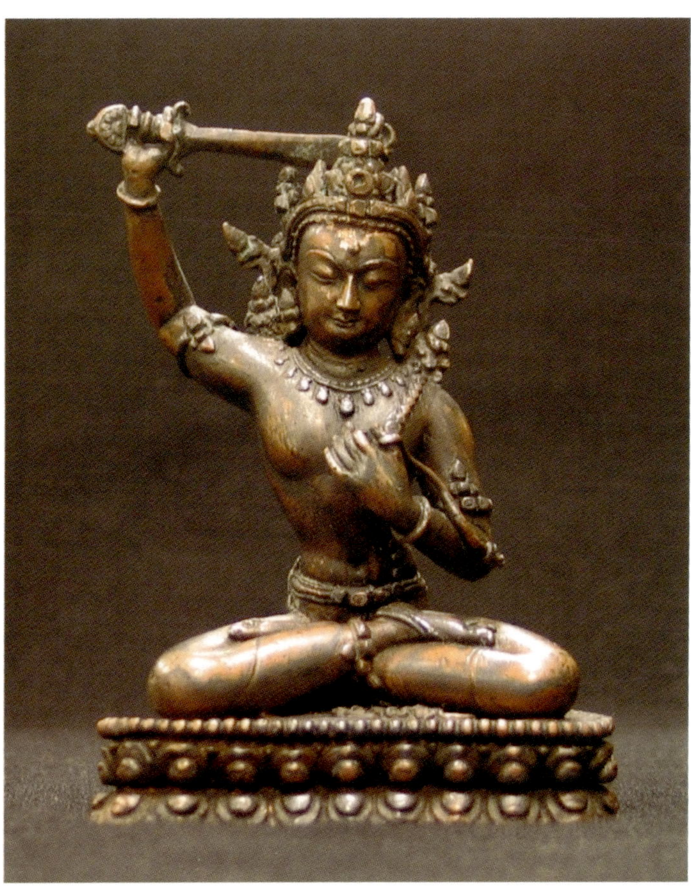

Manjushri
Tibet; 15th century
Copper alloy

Rubin Museum of Art
C2006.23.2 (HAR 65656)

Every aspect of life is addressed through Buddhist teachings, which are meant to be practiced continuously. Mastery over them is developed through habituation and intense contemplation where the artwork, as a basis, is brought to life through a series of meditative visualizations. The repeated practice of these principles is carried outward into daily life, not merely experienced during meditation sessions. Wisdom, clarity, the interconnectedness of all things, compassion for all beings, and a sense of profound peace all reveal themselves through vigilant practice and application.

It could be said that the complexity of Tibet's art developed in stark contrast to the vast, immense, and beautifully unusual exterior Tibetan landscape. In Tibet, stunning wide meadows abound, framed with enormous clear lakes and enclosed by towering snow-capped

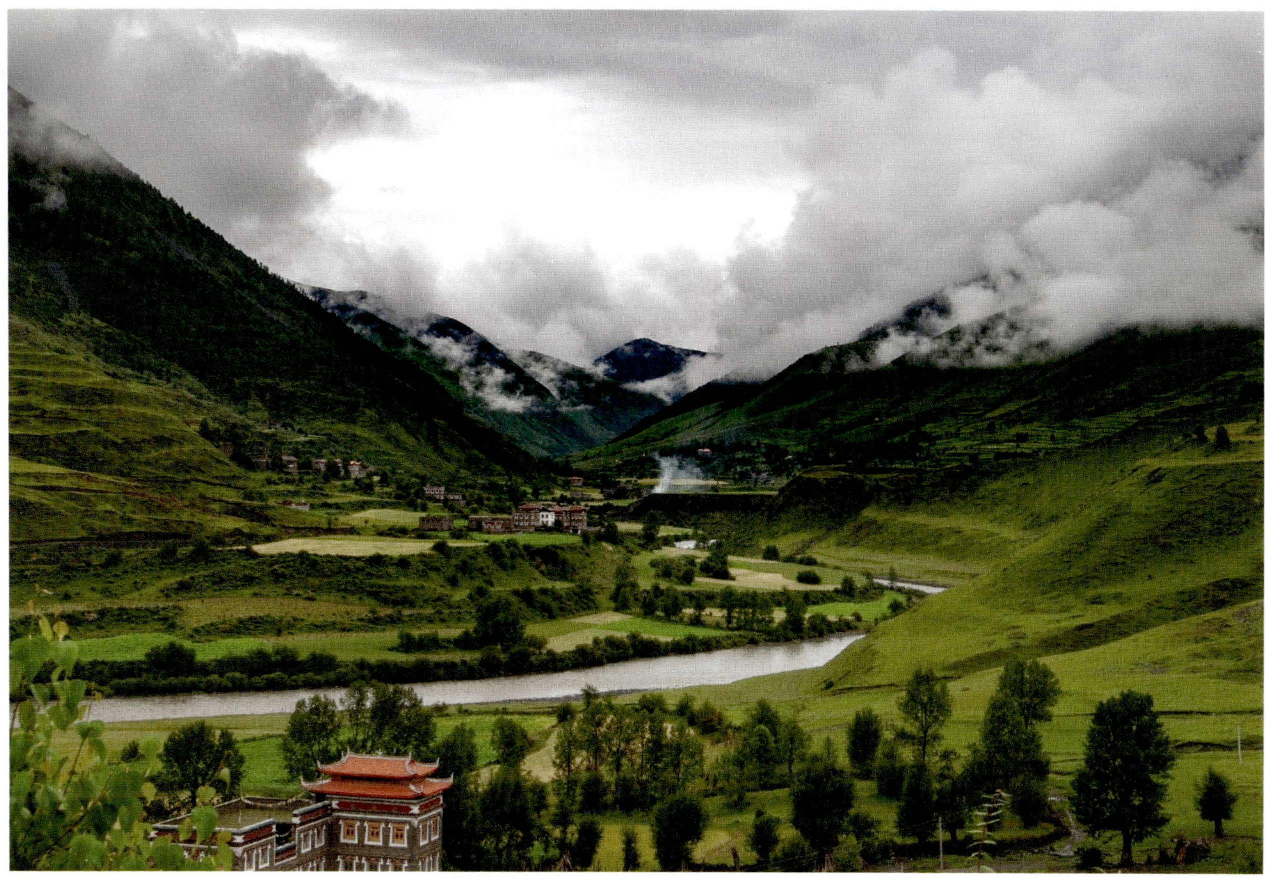

A lush valley in the Minyak region of Kham, on the eastern edge of the Tibetan Plateau

Photo: Bradley Aaron

mountains. These landscapes thematically oppose the intricate and minutely detailed artwork contained within Tibetan homes and temples. Living in a country with wide open plains and relatively few people, the Tibetans may have needed the complexity of their artwork as a balance to a nomadic existence or a life of farming—much simpler lives in comparison to our bustling existence in the West.

Nowadays, the meditation tradition has woven its way into the fabric of life here in the US. Because of the deeply connected roots of meditation and art in Tibet, it is no surprise that Western art museums have begun to use meditation as a means to enhance viewers' experience of art. However, the circumstances are different. Unlike Tibetans, we do not live in a vast and lowly populated plain; most of us are neither farmers nor nomads. We often suffer from too much complexity and are looking to simultaneously decrease stress and improve our performance, itself a seeming contradiction. And yet the popularity of meditation reflects a yearning for inner peace, ease, and comfort, and an acknowledgement of our interconnectedness, as well as a means to increase kindness and compassion. Is this a reflection of universal values amidst cultural differences?

Furthermore, the West has been contemplating its own art for a long time. While we do not approach art with the goal-oriented precision with which Tibetans approach their contemplations, it is common to ponder its meaning, wondering what the artist intended for us to know, understand, and experience. The West also has a long tradition of religious art, rich with symbolism and meaning, reflecting societal values and beliefs.

As Western contemplative practices become prevalent, it seems that we share the same goals as the Tibetans: to see, know, and experience the world in a different way—to change our view. As we tune in to our individual perception and awareness, we also hope to develop outwardly as more thoughtful and perceptive people. While contemplation can definitely help art students understand art, it may also help all of us to explore our own values, to have a more expansive view, and to develop ourselves in a variety of possibilities.

> "The exercises guided me to relate my personal experiences to the work of art presented. It gave me a much more in-depth understanding of the art."
>
> — **Rhetta Bearden,** *Looking Inward* participant

Earlier this year, The Fralin Museum of Art at the University of Virginia launched a new program, *Looking Inward,* that explored the application of meditation to art via guided contemplative art tours. To do so, a scholar of Tibetan Buddhism and Hinduism teamed with The Fralin's education staff. Based on what we saw in the artworks, combined with historical information about the artists' intentions, our skills in art history and criticism, and the contemplative techniques of Tibet and India, we created a meditative experience to guide looking at art. *Allegory with Cupid and Putti* (see page 57) was one of the pieces we contemplated at The Fralin. The artist's intention for this piece was the moral instruction of the viewer. Using contemplation to increase our perception and awareness, we considered the different themes, including the connection between love and creativity, the ephemerality of good deeds and time, and death.

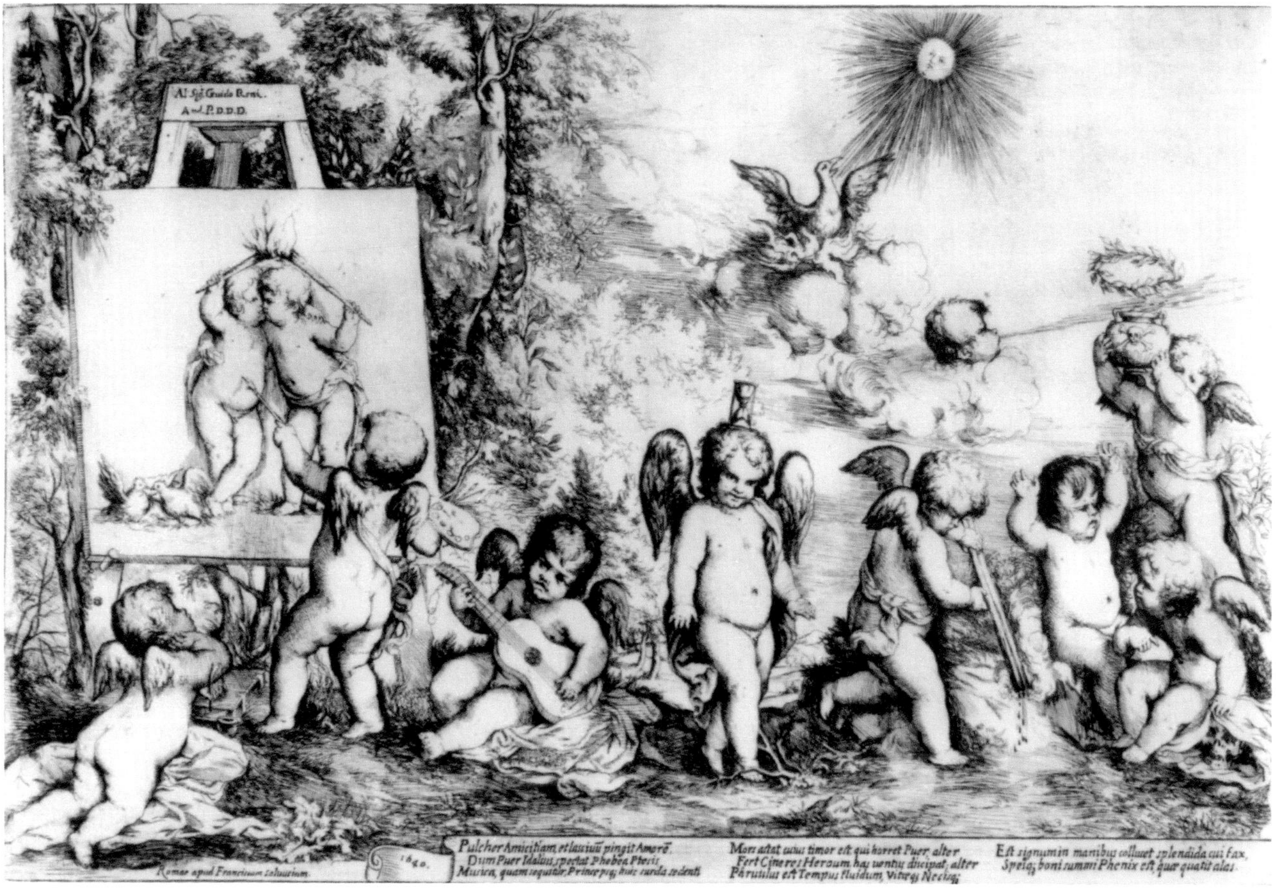

Giovanni Andrea Podestà
c. 1608–1673, Italian
Allegory with Cupid and Putti, 1640

While the contemplations themselves were sourced in the East, the pieces we used were American and European in origin and had messages and values in accordance with Western culture. In application, the contemplation touched on topics such as an expansion of how we see and interpret the world; the generation of love, compassion, joy, and equanimity; an analysis of what is love; and the relationship between love and creativity in our lives. We came out transformed, even if only a little, and saw things with new eyes.

---

1 Laird, Thomas. *The Story of Tibet: Conversations with the Dalai Lama.* New York: Grove Press, 2006; 27–41.

2 Della Santina, Peter, 2015. "The Development and Symbolism of Tibetan Buddhist Art and Iconography," http://www.himalayanart.org/pages/peter_della_santina/development_pdsantina.html.

The Space of Contemplation

by
William Sherman
Founding Director, OpenGrounds, Associate Vice President for Research, and Professor of Architecture

If an architect were to design a space for contemplation, what would be its characteristics? The question contains layers of presumptions, from the nature of contemplation to the agency of architecture in the support of any specific behavior. There is a common belief in the contemplative quality of an abstract space, one stripped of competing sensory stimuli—a place apart from the busyness of daily life—allowing a suspension of time which in turn opens the mind to focus. In such spaces, often associated with sacred or spiritual aspirations, particular phenomena may be heightened as objects for perception: the passage of projected sunlight, a distinctive acoustic property, or a singular scent. These have been the tools of religious architecture across many cultures for centuries.

> Plensa's installations for the Isola di San Georgio Maggiore are testament to his acute understanding of space and scale. His sculptures do not impose themselves on these historic spaces; rather they capture and reflect the actual light and shadows within to communicate a metaphorical language...they draw our attention to a world where migration and difference challenge civilised behaviour.... Plensa's work will connect people of many faiths and of no faith.
>
> — **Clare Lilley,** Director of Programmes at Yorkshire Sculpture Park

There is an emotional power to such spaces, inviting an individual immersion or a sense of community through shared experience. These spaces are designed specifically with the intent of causing a particular response, but one must be careful in presuming a universality to their power. The response to architectural space is highly intersubjective, and therefore highly contingent: while there may be general characteristics of a peaceful, contemplative environment, individual responses to a particular place are dependent upon many factors including cultural framework, life experience, temporal sequences, and preparation of the mind of the viewer. A particular space may favor a general form of response, but contemplation is a conscious act, often focused on a deep connection to a particular object, piercing the boundary between object and subject. In the presentation of icons and artifacts for spiritual reflection—another long tradition of sacred architecture—one may find an equally valid approach to the conception of a space for contemplation. In such a space, the artifact initiates an exploration of the self by reflection in the work; the presentation of the work, the quality of its making, and the meaning it conveys serve as a gateway to both a world beyond and a world within.

As works of art moved from a sacred context to the secular realm, in subject and site, the museum has emerged as the locus for a new form of contemplation. It is here that the

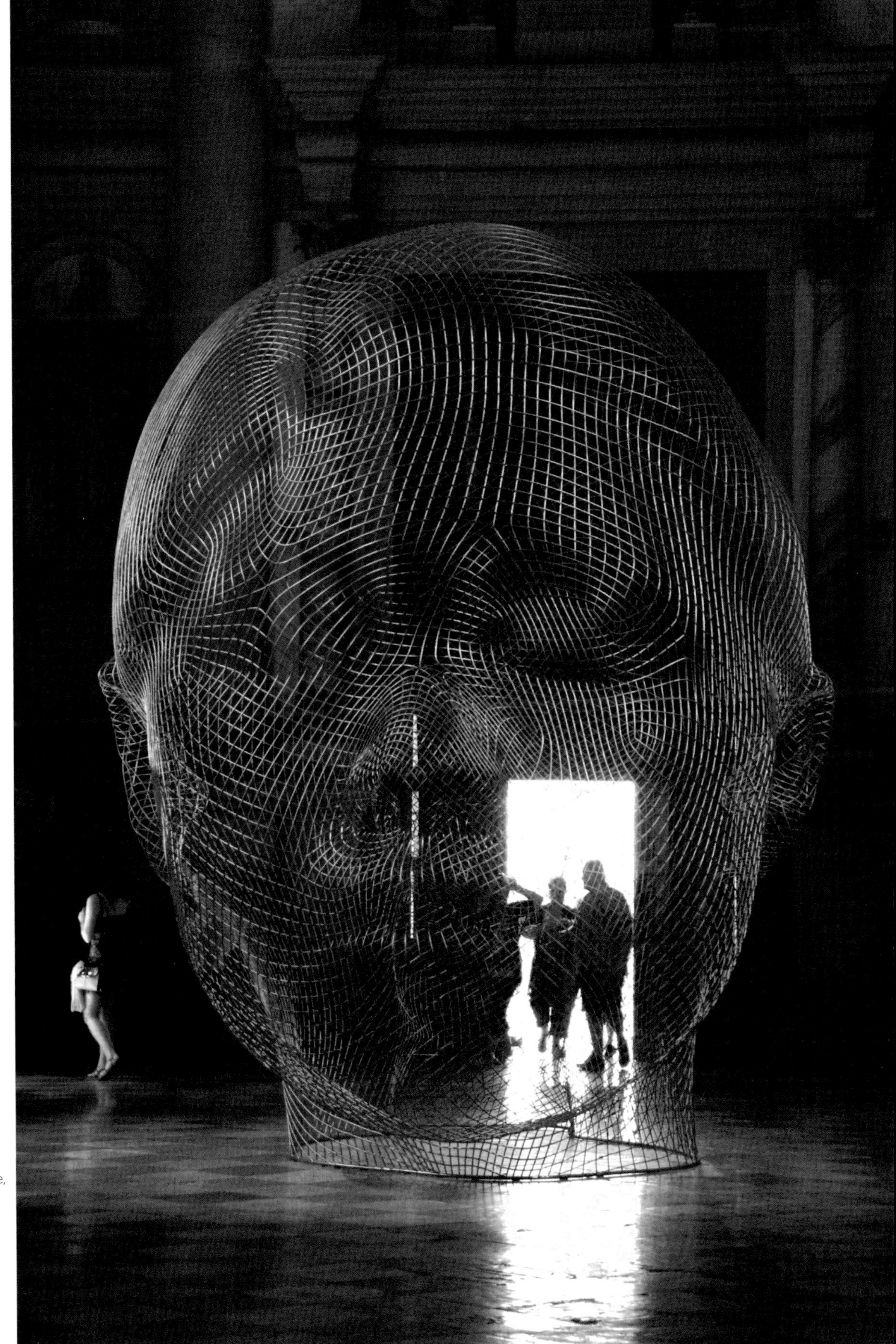

Sculpture
Jaume Plensa
Spanish, b. 1955
Together. Stainless Steel

Location
Church of San Giorgio Maggiore,
Venice, 2015

Photo: William Sherman

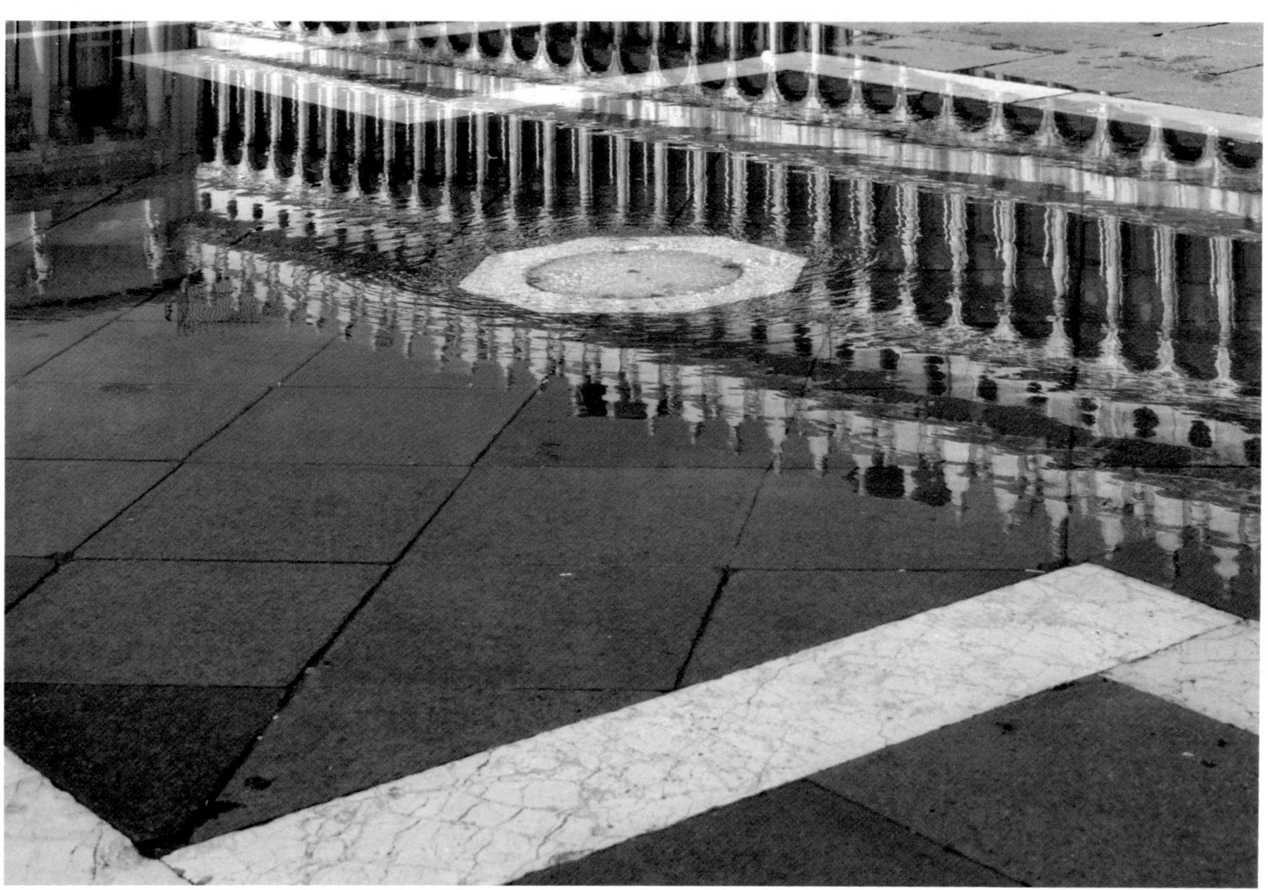

Acqua alta in Piazza San Marco, Venice
Photo: William Sherman

phenomenal and the representational intersect, the task of the curator being to distinguish a work of art, and the admiration it elicits, from an ordinary object for consumption—to prolong the viewing and thus to give the viewer sufficient time to engage deeply in the work. In that process, one may move beyond the "studium" of the work, a term Roland Barthes defines, in his brilliant essay on photography, *Camera Lucida*,[1] as the arena in which the viewer appreciates the art historical significance of the work, and perceives a dimension of the artist's intent as well as the devices employed to achieve a desired result. The *studium* resides within the work itself, rather than in the eye of the beholder. Barthes defines the next layer of engagement as the "punctum," the piercing detail or quality that moves us, that draws us back in, perhaps even later when the work is no longer present but continues to haunt. The *punctum* is a product of contingency, a focus on the singular quality of a work that has particular individual meaning, and it is found in the relationship between work and viewer, not solely in the work itself. It requires attention to recognize this possibility, the moment when the distance between subject and object collapses and a space opens up for extended reflection, a duration filled by contemplation. The sense of the *punctum* and the act of contemplation are linked as ruptures in time. The architecture of the space of contemplation facilitates that opening.

The connection of this heightened state of awareness to human wellness has long roots in theory, philosophy, and sacred belief—in the link between the good and the beautiful in classical philosophy and architectural treatises, in the restorative power of nature in the Romantic landscape, in the instrumentality of modern architecture to cleanse the industrial city's pestilent fabric. The testing of these constructs through measurements of nuanced physiological response or comprehensive statistical patterns has only recently become possible. Measurable connections are being made between mental states and physiological processes; between capacities to focus and diagnostic skills; between deep engagement with a painting, or with music, and stress levels; between an accessible landscape and public health. This is the frontier of an emerging form of design and art practice, in which demonstrable effects on human wellness are part of the artistic intent. Music and drawing rewire the brain as they recalibrate the body's systems. The contemplation of art alters the metabolism. The space of this experience has the capacity to pierce the cultural frame, catalyzing an engagement between the self and the world. With this greater understanding, wellness takes on a new meaning at the intersection of art, theory, cultural practice, and science, embracing the complexity and interconnectedness of the manifold dimensions of our humanity.

The collaboration between the University of Virginia, The Phillips Collection, and the National Academy of Sciences that is represented here grows out of this shared understanding. For institutions with a common commitment to advancing a deeper knowledge of the world, there is a tremendous opportunity to stretch into new territory through sustained dialogue and experimentation. The differences in methods, intellectual frameworks, modes of communication, and modes of reasoning can, in the right setting and with shared purpose, be catalysts for inspired experimentation and insight. It is out of these boundary-crossing partnerships that a deeper understanding of the connections between art, contemplation, and wellness will emerge.

1 Barthes, Roland. *Camera Lucida: Reflections on Photography,* trans. Richard Howard. New York: Hill and Wang, 1980.

Acknowledgements

As we come to the end of this project—our third OpenGrounds publication, and the second in our "Changing Views" series—we are once again struck by the incredible results of collaboration. From our initial conversation with The Phillips Collection and National Academy of Sciences, when we recognized a mutual interest in the theme of *Art, Contemplation, and Wellness,* to the many events that helped us explore the theme in various ways, to essays that have been written for this publication, we are deeply grateful for the wealth of knowledge and experience of the contributors who have made this project possible.

We extend special thanks to The Phillips Collection, the instigator behind our exploration of art, contemplation, and wellness. It has been a joy and honor to work with Brooke Rosenblatt and Klaus Ottmann on the development of the contemplative audio tour, our multiple collaborative events, and this publication.

A huge thank you to JD Talasek, the fantastic director of Cultural Programs of the National Academy of Sciences, whose invitation to present at a DC Art Science Evening Rendezvous (DASER) event provided a consistent fuel to propel the collaboration forward, and a clear outcome towards which we were working.

Thank you, also, to the faculty and staff at the University of Virginia without whose enthusiasm this project would not have come together: Barbara Bernstein, whose contemplative approach to drawing added an essential "hands-on" dimension to this initiative; Fred Everett Maus, who took us beyond visual arts into the rich world of music and consciousness; Marcia Day Childress, who helped to bring the medical community into this project; Jordan Love and the entire staff at The Fralin Museum of Art, whose openness to these ideas was key to the project's success; David Germano and Erin Hall, from the Contemplative Sciences Center, who brought a depth of experience and expertise to the table; Naomi Worth, who was willing to explore a new and unprecedented partnership; and Dorrie Fontaine, whose visionary approach to compassionate care has been an essential catalyst for UVA's interest in contemplation. And of course, we extend our gratitude to the students and OpenGrounds interns who provided tremendous help along the way, especially Caroline Nilsson, Holly Zajur, Claire Constance, Stephanie Katsias, and Juliana Echeverri.

For their crucial role in the completion of this publication, we would like to thank Anne Chesnut, our incredible graphic designer and long-time collaborator; and Margo Browning, our astute copy editor.

Finally, we are deeply indebted to the Arts Council for their generous support of OpenGrounds and the *Art, Contemplation, and Wellness* initiative.

OpenGrounds, University of Virginia
PO Box 800317
Charlottesville VA 22908-0317
opengrounds.virginia.edu

ISBN 978-0-9893995-2-4

Colophon

Designer
Anne Chesnut
Charlottesville VA

Managing editor
Lindsey Hepler
Charlottesville VA

Copy editor
Margo Browning
Charlottesville VA

Printer
Worth Higgins & Associates, Inc.
Richmond VA

Stock
Endurance Silk Cover & Text

Type
Whitney